Mometrix
TEST PREPARATION

Series 24
Exam Secrets
Study Guide

D0074465

DEAR FUTURE EXAM SUCCESS STORY

First of all, **THANK YOU** for purchasing Mometrix study materials!

Second, congratulations! You are one of the few determined test-takers who are committed to doing whatever it takes to excel on your exam. **You have come to the right place.** We developed these study materials with one goal in mind: to deliver you the information you need in a format that's concise and easy to use.

In addition to optimizing your guide for the content of the test, we've outlined our recommended steps for breaking down the preparation process into small, attainable goals so you can make sure you stay on track.

We've also analyzed the entire test-taking process, identifying the most common pitfalls and showing how you can overcome them and be ready for any curveball the test throws you.

Standardized testing is one of the biggest obstacles on your road to success, which only increases the importance of doing well in the high-pressure, high-stakes environment of test day. Your results on this test could have a significant impact on your future, and this guide provides the information and practical advice to help you achieve your full potential on test day.

Your success is our success

We would love to hear from you! If you would like to share the story of your exam success or if you have any questions or comments in regard to our products, please contact us at **800-673-8175** or **support@mometrix.com**.

Thanks again for your business and we wish you continued success!

Sincerely,
The Mometrix Test Preparation Team

Need more help? Check out our flashcards at:
http://MometrixFlashcards.com/Series24

TABLE OF CONTENTS

Introduction

Thank you for purchasing this resource! You have made the choice to prepare yourself for a test that could have a huge impact on your future, and this guide is designed to help you be fully ready for test day. Obviously, it's important to have a solid understanding of the test material, but you also need to be prepared for the unique environment and stressors of the test, so that you can perform to the best of your abilities.

For this purpose, the first section that appears in this guide is the **Secret Keys**. We've devoted countless hours to meticulously researching what works and what doesn't, and we've boiled down our findings to the five most impactful steps you can take to improve your performance on the test. We start at the beginning with study planning and move through the preparation process, all the way to the testing strategies that will help you get the most out of what you know when you're finally sitting in front of the test.

We recommend that you start preparing for your test as far in advance as possible. However, if you've bought this guide as a last-minute study resource and only have a few days before your test, we recommend that you skip over the first two Secret Keys since they address a long-term study plan.

If you struggle with **test anxiety**, we strongly encourage you to check out our recommendations for how you can overcome it. Test anxiety is a formidable foe, but it can be beaten, and we want to make sure you have the tools you need to defeat it.

Secret Key #1 – Plan Big, Study Small

There's a lot riding on your performance. If you want to ace this test, you're going to need to keep your skills sharp and the material fresh in your mind. You need a plan that lets you review everything you need to know while still fitting in your schedule. We'll break this strategy down into three categories.

Information Organization

Start with the information you already have: the official test outline. From this, you can make a complete list of all the concepts you need to cover before the test. Organize these concepts into groups that can be studied together, and create a list of any related vocabulary you need to learn so you can brush up on any difficult terms. You'll want to keep this vocabulary list handy once you actually start studying since you may need to add to it along the way.

Time Management

Once you have your set of study concepts, decide how to spread them out over the time you have left before the test. Break your study plan into small, clear goals so you have a manageable task for each day and know exactly what you're doing. Then just focus on one small step at a time. When you manage your time this way, you don't need to spend hours at a time studying. Studying a small block of content for a short period each day helps you retain information better and avoid stressing over how much you have left to do. You can relax knowing that you have a plan to cover everything in time. In order for this strategy to be effective though, you have to start studying early and stick to your schedule. Avoid the exhaustion and futility that comes from last-minute cramming!

Study Environment

The environment you study in has a big impact on your learning. Studying in a coffee shop, while probably more enjoyable, is not likely to be as fruitful as studying in a quiet room. It's important to keep distractions to a minimum. You're only planning to study for a short block of time, so make the most of it. Don't pause to check your phone or get up to find a snack. It's also important to **avoid multitasking**. Research has consistently shown that multitasking will make your studying dramatically less effective. Your study area should also be comfortable and well-lit so you don't have the distraction of straining your eyes or sitting on an uncomfortable chair.

 The time of day you study is also important. You want to be rested and alert. Don't wait until just before bedtime. Study when you'll be most likely to comprehend and remember. Even better, if you know what time of day your test will be, set that time aside for study. That way your brain will be used to working on that subject at that specific time and you'll have a better chance of recalling information.

Finally, it can be helpful to team up with others who are studying for the same test. Your actual studying should be done in as isolated an environment as possible, but the work of organizing the information and setting up the study plan can be divided up. In between study sessions, you can discuss with your teammates the concepts that you're all studying and quiz each other on the details. Just be sure that your teammates are as serious about the test as you are. If you find that your study time is being replaced with social time, you might need to find a new team.

2

Secret Key #2 – Make Your Studying Count

You're devoting a lot of time and effort to preparing for this test, so you want to be absolutely certain it will pay off. This means doing more than just reading the content and hoping you can remember it on test day. It's important to make every minute of study count. There are two main areas you can focus on to make your studying count.

Retention

It doesn't matter how much time you study if you can't remember the material. You need to make sure you are retaining the concepts. To check your retention of the information you're learning, try recalling it at later times with minimal prompting. Try carrying around flashcards and glance at one or two from time to time or ask a friend who's also studying for the test to quiz you.

To enhance your retention, look for ways to put the information into practice so that you can apply it rather than simply recalling it. If you're using the information in practical ways, it will be much easier to remember. Similarly, it helps to solidify a concept in your mind if you're not only reading it to yourself but also explaining it to someone else. Ask a friend to let you teach them about a concept you're a little shaky on (or speak aloud to an imaginary audience if necessary). As you try to summarize, define, give examples, and answer your friend's questions, you'll understand the concepts better and they will stay with you longer. Finally, step back for a big picture view and ask yourself how each piece of information fits with the whole subject. When you link the different concepts together and see them working together as a whole, it's easier to remember the individual components.

Finally, practice showing your work on any multi-step problems, even if you're just studying. Writing out each step you take to solve a problem will help solidify the process in your mind, and you'll be more likely to remember it during the test.

Modality

Modality simply refers to the means or method by which you study. Choosing a study modality that fits your own individual learning style is crucial. No two people learn best in exactly the same way, so it's important to know your strengths and use them to your advantage.

For example, if you learn best by visualization, focus on visualizing a concept in your mind and draw an image or a diagram. Try color-coding your notes, illustrating them, or creating symbols that will trigger your mind to recall a learned concept. If you learn best by hearing or discussing information, find a study partner who learns the same way or read aloud to yourself. Think about how to put the information in your own words. Imagine that you are giving a lecture on the topic and record yourself so you can listen to it later.

For any learning style, flashcards can be helpful. Organize the information so you can take advantage of spare moments to review. Underline key words or phrases. Use different colors for different categories. Mnemonic devices (such as creating a short list in which every item starts with the same letter) can also help with retention. Find what works best for you and use it to store the information in your mind most effectively and easily.

3

Secret Key #3 – Practice the Right Way

Your success on test day depends not only on how many hours you put into preparing, but also on whether you prepared the right way. It's good to check along the way to see if your studying is paying off. One of the most effective ways to do this is by taking practice tests to evaluate your progress. Practice tests are useful because they show exactly where you need to improve. Every time you take a practice test, pay special attention to these three groups of questions:

- The questions you got wrong
- The questions you had to guess on, even if you guessed right
- The questions you found difficult or slow to work through

This will show you exactly what your weak areas are, and where you need to devote more study time. Ask yourself why each of these questions gave you trouble. Was it because you didn't understand the material? Was it because you didn't remember the vocabulary? Do you need more repetitions on this type of question to build speed and confidence? Dig into those questions and figure out how you can strengthen your weak areas as you go back to review the material.

 Additionally, many practice tests have a section explaining the answer choices. It can be tempting to read the explanation and think that you now have a good understanding of the concept. However, an explanation likely only covers part of the question's broader context. Even if the explanation makes perfect sense, **go back and investigate** every concept related to the question until you're positive you have a thorough understanding.

As you go along, keep in mind that the practice test is just that: practice. Memorizing these questions and answers will not be very helpful on the actual test because it is unlikely to have any of the same exact questions. If you only know the right answers to the sample questions, you won't be prepared for the real thing. **Study the concepts** until you understand them fully, and then you'll be able to answer any question that shows up on the test.

It's important to wait on the practice tests until you're ready. If you take a test on your first day of study, you may be overwhelmed by the amount of material covered and how much you need to learn. Work up to it gradually.

On test day, you'll need to be prepared for answering questions, managing your time, and using the test-taking strategies you've learned. It's a lot to balance, like a mental marathon that will have a big impact on your future. Like training for a marathon, you'll need to start slowly and work your way up. When test day arrives, you'll be ready.

Start with the strategies you've read in the first two Secret Keys—plan your course and study in the way that works best for you. If you have time, consider using multiple study resources to get different approaches to the same concepts. It can be helpful to see difficult concepts from more than one angle. Then find a good source for practice tests. Many times, the test website will suggest potential study resources or provide sample tests.

Practice Test Strategy

If you're able to find at least three practice tests, we recommend this strategy:

UNTIMED AND OPEN-BOOK PRACTICE

Take the first test with no time constraints and with your notes and study guide handy. Take your time and focus on applying the strategies you've learned.

TIMED AND OPEN-BOOK PRACTICE

Take the second practice test open-book as well, but set a timer and practice pacing yourself to finish in time.

TIMED AND CLOSED-BOOK PRACTICE

Take any other practice tests as if it were test day. Set a timer and put away your study materials. Sit at a table or desk in a quiet room, imagine yourself at the testing center, and answer questions as quickly and accurately as possible.

Keep repeating timed and closed-book tests on a regular basis until you run out of practice tests or it's time for the actual test. Your mind will be ready for the schedule and stress of test day, and you'll be able to focus on recalling the material you've learned.

Secret Key #4 – Pace Yourself

Once you're fully prepared for the material on the test, your biggest challenge on test day will be managing your time. Just knowing that the clock is ticking can make you panic even if you have plenty of time left. Work on pacing yourself so you can build confidence against the time constraints of the exam. Pacing is a difficult skill to master, especially in a high-pressure environment, so **practice is vital**.

Set time expectations for your pace based on how much time is available. For example, if a section has 60 questions and the time limit is 30 minutes, you know you have to average 30 seconds or less per question in order to answer them all. Although 30 seconds is the hard limit, set 25 seconds per question as your goal, so you reserve extra time to spend on harder questions. When you budget extra time for the harder questions, you no longer have any reason to stress when those questions take longer to answer.

Don't let this time expectation distract you from working through the test at a calm, steady pace, but keep it in mind so you don't spend too much time on any one question. Recognize that taking extra time on one question you don't understand may keep you from answering two that you do understand later in the test. If your time limit for a question is up and you're still not sure of the answer, mark it and move on, and come back to it later if the time and the test format allow. If the testing format doesn't allow you to return to earlier questions, just make an educated guess; then put it out of your mind and move on.

On the easier questions, be careful not to rush. It may seem wise to hurry through them so you have more time for the challenging ones, but it's not worth missing one if you know the concept and just didn't take the time to read the question fully. Work efficiently but make sure you understand the question and have looked at all of the answer choices, since more than one may seem right at first.

Even if you're paying attention to the time, you may find yourself a little behind at some point. You should speed up to get back on track, but do so wisely. Don't panic; just take a few seconds less on each question until you're caught up. Don't guess without thinking, but do look through the answer choices and eliminate any you know are wrong. If you can get down to two choices, it is often worthwhile to guess from those. Once you've chosen an answer, move on and don't dwell on any that you skipped or had to hurry through. If a question was taking too long, chances are it was one of the harder ones, so you weren't as likely to get it right anyway.

On the other hand, if you find yourself getting ahead of schedule, it may be beneficial to slow down a little. The more quickly you work, the more likely you are to make a careless mistake that will affect your score. You've budgeted time for each question, so don't be afraid to spend that time. Practice an efficient but careful pace to get the most out of the time you have.

Secret Key #5 – Have a Plan for Guessing

When you're taking the test, you may find yourself stuck on a question. Some of the answer choices seem better than others, but you don't see the one answer choice that is obviously correct. What do you do?

The scenario described above is very common, yet most test takers have not effectively prepared for it. Developing and practicing a plan for guessing may be one of the single most effective uses of your time as you get ready for the exam.

In developing your plan for guessing, there are three questions to address:

- When should you start the guessing process?
- How should you narrow down the choices?
- Which answer should you choose?

When to Start the Guessing Process

Unless your plan for guessing is to select C every time (which, despite its merits, is not what we recommend), you need to leave yourself enough time to apply your answer elimination strategies. Since you have a limited amount of time for each question, that means that if you're going to give yourself the best shot at guessing correctly, you have to decide quickly whether or not you will guess.

Of course, the best-case scenario is that you don't have to guess at all, so first, see if you can answer the question based on your knowledge of the subject and basic reasoning skills. Focus on the key words in the question and try to jog your memory of related topics. Give yourself a chance to bring the knowledge to mind, but once you realize that you don't have (or you can't access) the knowledge you need to answer the question, it's time to start the guessing process.

It's almost always better to start the guessing process too early than too late. It only takes a few seconds to remember something and answer the question from knowledge. Carefully eliminating wrong answer choices takes longer. Plus, going through the process of eliminating answer choices can actually help jog your memory.

Summary: Start the guessing process as soon as you decide that you can't answer the question based on your knowledge.

7

How to Narrow Down the Choices

The next chapter in this book (**Test-Taking Strategies**) includes a wide range of strategies for how to approach questions and how to look for answer choices to eliminate. You will definitely want to read those carefully, practice them, and figure out which ones work best for you. Here though, we're going to address a mindset rather than a particular strategy.

Your odds of guessing an answer correctly depend on how many options you are choosing from.

Number of options left	5	4	3	2	1
Odds of guessing correctly	20%	25%	33%	50%	100%

You can see from this chart just how valuable it is to be able to eliminate incorrect answers and make an educated guess, but there are two things that many test takers do that cause them to miss out on the benefits of guessing:

- Accidentally eliminating the correct answer
- Selecting an answer based on an impression

We'll look at the first one here, and the second one in the next section.

To avoid accidentally eliminating the correct answer, we recommend a thought exercise called **the $5 challenge**. In this challenge, you only eliminate an answer choice from contention if you are willing to bet $5 on it being wrong. Why $5? Five dollars is a small but not insignificant amount of money. It's an amount you could afford to lose but wouldn't want to throw away. And while losing

$5 once might not hurt too much, doing it twenty times will set you back $100. In the same way, each small decision you make—eliminating a choice here, guessing on a question there—won't by itself impact your score very much, but when you put them all together, they can make a big difference. By holding each answer choice elimination decision to a higher standard, you can reduce the risk of accidentally eliminating the correct answer.

The $5 challenge can also be applied in a positive sense: If you are willing to bet $5 that an answer choice *is* correct, go ahead and mark it as correct.

Summary: Only eliminate an answer choice if you are willing to bet $5 that it is wrong.

8

Which Answer to Choose

You're taking the test. You've run into a hard question and decided you'll have to guess. You've eliminated all the answer choices you're willing to bet $5 on. Now you have to pick an answer. Why do we even need to talk about this? Why can't you just pick whichever one you feel like when the time comes?

The answer to these questions is that if you don't come into the test with a plan, you'll rely on your impression to select an answer choice, and if you do that, you risk falling into a trap. The test writers know that everyone who takes their test will be guessing on some of the questions, so they intentionally write wrong answer choices to seem plausible. You still have to pick an answer though, and if the wrong answer choices are designed to look right, how can you ever be sure that you're not falling for their trap? The best solution we've found to this dilemma is to take the decision out of your hands entirely. Here is the process we recommend:

Once you've eliminated any choices that you are confident (willing to bet $5) are wrong, select the first remaining choice as your answer.

Whether you choose to select the first remaining choice, the second, or the last, the important thing is that you use some preselected standard. Using this approach guarantees that you will not be enticed into selecting an answer choice that looks right, because you are not basing your decision on how the answer choices look.

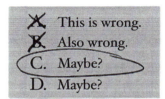

This is not meant to make you question your knowledge. Instead, it is to help you recognize the difference between your knowledge and your impressions. There's a huge difference between thinking an answer is right because of what you know, and thinking an answer is right because it looks or sounds like it should be right.

Summary: To ensure that your selection is appropriately random, make a predetermined selection from among all answer choices you have not eliminated.

Test-Taking Strategies

This section contains a list of test-taking strategies that you may find helpful as you work through the test. By taking what you know and applying logical thought, you can maximize your chances of answering any question correctly!

It is very important to realize that every question is different and every person is different: no single strategy will work on every question, and no single strategy will work for every person. That's why we've included all of them here, so you can try them out and determine which ones work best for different types of questions and which ones work best for you.

Question Strategies

☑ READ CAREFULLY

Read the question and the answer choices carefully. Don't miss the question because you misread the terms. You have plenty of time to read each question thoroughly and make sure you understand what is being asked. Yet a happy medium must be attained, so don't waste too much time. You must read carefully and efficiently.

☑ CONTEXTUAL CLUES

Look for contextual clues. If the question includes a word you are not familiar with, look at the immediate context for some indication of what the word might mean. Contextual clues can often give you all the information you need to decipher the meaning of an unfamiliar word. Even if you can't determine the meaning, you may be able to narrow down the possibilities enough to make a solid guess at the answer to the question.

☑ PREFIXES

If you're having trouble with a word in the question or answer choices, try dissecting it. Take advantage of every clue that the word might include. Prefixes and suffixes can be a huge help. Usually, they allow you to determine a basic meaning. *Pre-* means before, *post-* means after, *pro-* is positive, *de-* is negative. From prefixes and suffixes, you can get an idea of the general meaning of the word and try to put it into context.

☑ HEDGE WORDS

Watch out for critical hedge words, such as *likely, may, can, sometimes, often, almost, mostly, usually, generally, rarely,* and *sometimes.* Question writers insert these hedge phrases to cover every possibility. Often an answer choice will be wrong simply because it leaves no room for exception. Be on guard for answer choices that have definitive words such as *exactly* and *always.*

☑ SWITCHBACK WORDS

Stay alert for *switchbacks.* These are the words and phrases frequently used to alert you to shifts in thought. The most common switchback words are *but, although,* and *however.* Others include *nevertheless, on the other hand, even though, while, in spite of, despite,* and *regardless of.* Switchback words are important to catch because they can change the direction of the question or an answer choice.

⊘ Face Value

When in doubt, use common sense. Accept the situation in the problem at face value. Don't read too much into it. These problems will not require you to make wild assumptions. If you have to go beyond creativity and warp time or space in order to have an answer choice fit the question, then you should move on and consider the other answer choices. These are normal problems rooted in reality. The applicable relationship or explanation may not be readily apparent, but it is there for you to figure out. Use your common sense to interpret anything that isn't clear.

Answer Choice Strategies

⊘ Answer Selection

The most thorough way to pick an answer choice is to identify and eliminate wrong answers until only one is left, then confirm it is the correct answer. Sometimes an answer choice may immediately seem right, but be careful. The test writers will usually put more than one reasonable answer choice on each question, so take a second to read all of them and make sure that the other choices are not equally obvious. As long as you have time left, it is better to read every answer choice than to pick the first one that looks right without checking the others.

⊘ Answer Choice Families

An answer choice family consists of two (in rare cases, three) answer choices that are very similar in construction and cannot all be true at the same time. If you see two answer choices that are direct opposites or parallels, one of them is usually the correct answer. For instance, if one answer choice says that quantity x increases and another either says that quantity x decreases (opposite) or says that quantity y increases (parallel), then those answer choices would fall into the same family. An answer choice that doesn't match the construction of the answer choice family is more likely to be incorrect. Most questions will not have answer choice families, but when they do appear, you should be prepared to recognize them.

⊘ Eliminate Answers

Eliminate answer choices as soon as you realize they are wrong, but make sure you consider all possibilities. If you are eliminating answer choices and realize that the last one you are left with is also wrong, don't panic. Start over and consider each choice again. There may be something you missed the first time that you will realize on the second pass.

⊘ Avoid Fact Traps

Don't be distracted by an answer choice that is factually true but doesn't answer the question. You are looking for the choice that answers the question. Stay focused on what the question is asking for so you don't accidentally pick an answer that is true but incorrect. Always go back to the question and make sure the answer choice you've selected actually answers the question and is not merely a true statement.

⊘ Extreme Statements

In general, you should avoid answers that put forth extreme actions as standard practice or proclaim controversial ideas as established fact. An answer choice that states the "process should be used in certain situations, if…" is much more likely to be correct than one that states the "process should be discontinued completely." The first is a calm rational statement and doesn't even make a definitive, uncompromising stance, using a hedge word *if* to provide wiggle room, whereas the second choice is far more extreme.

⊘ Benchmark

As you read through the answer choices and you come across one that seems to answer the question well, mentally select that answer choice. This is not your final answer, but it's the one that will help you evaluate the other answer choices. The one that you selected is your benchmark or standard for judging each of the other answer choices. Every other answer choice must be compared to your benchmark. That choice is correct until proven otherwise by another answer choice beating it. If you find a better answer, then that one becomes your new benchmark. Once you've decided that no other choice answers the question as well as your benchmark, you have your final answer.

⊘ Predict the Answer

Before you even start looking at the answer choices, it is often best to try to predict the answer. When you come up with the answer on your own, it is easier to avoid distractions and traps because you will know exactly what to look for. The right answer choice is unlikely to be word-for-word what you came up with, but it should be a close match. Even if you are confident that you have the right answer, you should still take the time to read each option before moving on.

General Strategies

⊘ Tough Questions

If you are stumped on a problem or it appears too hard or too difficult, don't waste time. Move on! Remember though, if you can quickly check for obviously incorrect answer choices, your chances of guessing correctly are greatly improved. Before you completely give up, at least try to knock out a couple of possible answers. Eliminate what you can and then guess at the remaining answer choices before moving on.

⊘ Check Your Work

Since you will probably not know every term listed and the answer to every question, it is important that you get credit for the ones that you do know. Don't miss any questions through careless mistakes. If at all possible, try to take a second to look back over your answer selection and make sure you've selected the correct answer choice and haven't made a costly careless mistake (such as marking an answer choice that you didn't mean to mark). This quick double check should more than pay for itself in caught mistakes for the time it costs.

⊘ Pace Yourself

It's easy to be overwhelmed when you're looking at a page full of questions; your mind is confused and full of random thoughts, and the clock is ticking down faster than you would like. Calm down and maintain the pace that you have set for yourself. Especially as you get down to the last few minutes of the test, don't let the small numbers on the clock make you panic. As long as you are on track by monitoring your pace, you are guaranteed to have time for each question.

⊘ Don't Rush

It is very easy to make errors when you are in a hurry. Maintaining a fast pace in answering questions is pointless if it makes you miss questions that you would have gotten right otherwise. Test writers like to include distracting information and wrong answers that seem right. Taking a little extra time to avoid careless mistakes can make all the difference in your test score. Find a pace that allows you to be confident in the answers that you select.

12

⊘ KEEP MOVING

Panicking will not help you pass the test, so do your best to stay calm and keep moving. Taking deep breaths and going through the answer elimination steps you practiced can help to break through a stress barrier and keep your pace.

Final Notes

The combination of a solid foundation of content knowledge and the confidence that comes from practicing your plan for applying that knowledge is the key to maximizing your performance on test day. As your foundation of content knowledge is built up and strengthened, you'll find that the strategies included in this chapter become more and more effective in helping you quickly sift through the distractions and traps of the test to isolate the correct answer.

Now that you're preparing to move forward into the test content chapters of this book, be sure to keep your goal in mind. As you read, think about how you will be able to apply this information on the test. If you've already seen sample questions for the test and you have an idea of the question format and style, try to come up with questions of your own that you can answer based on what you're reading. This will give you valuable practice applying your knowledge in the same ways you can expect to on test day.

Good luck and good studying!

Supervision of Registration of the Broker-Dealer and Personnel Management Activities

ARTICLE 4 OF FINRA BY-LAWS

Application for membership (Section 1) - a signed application for membership is to be submitted electronically and it is to contain:

1. an agreement to comply with governing laws, rules, and regulations;
2. an agreement to pay dues, assessments, and other charges promptly;
3. and other reasonable information the Corporation requires.

Executive representative (Section 3) - a member is to appoint an executive representative who will represent, vote, and act on behalf of the member in all affairs of the Corporation.

Resignation of members (Section 5) - membership can be terminated by formal resignation. Such resignations are to be filled electronically, and will not take effect until 30 days after being received by the Corporation.

Retention of jurisdiction (Section 6) - a resigned member is still subject to the filing of a complaint under the Rule of the Corporation based on conduct that began prior to the resignation.

Transfer and termination of membership (Section 7) - membership cannot be transferred, and the membership of a business entity terminates upon its liquidation, dissolution, or winding up. A sole-proprietor's membership terminates at death. Consolidation, reorganization, merger, change of name, or other similar changes to not terminate membership, rather, the membership is transferred to the surviving entity deemed to be the successor.

Registration of branch offices (Section 8) - each member branch office is to be registered and listed on the membership roll of the Corporation and is to pay any dues, assessments, or other charges that may be fixed. A member is to notify the corporation promptly when a branch office is opened, closed, relocated, has a change in supervisor, or has a change in activities.

NYSE RULE 401A

Customer complaints (NYSE Rule 401A) - a member is to, for every customer complaint received, acknowledge receipt within 15 days and respond within a reasonable period of time. Acknowledgement and response must be either in writing sent through the mail, or sent to the email address from which the complaint was received. If the complaint was verbal, the response is either to be sent in the mail or given verbally and recorded in a log.

SECTION 3 OF THE SECURITIES EXCHANGE ACT

Statutory disqualification as per Section 3 of the Securities Exchange Act of 1934 applies to a person:

1. when he is expelled or suspended from membership or participation in any self-regulatory organization;
2. when the Commission or other regulatory agency denies or suspends registration as or association with a broker-dealer for a period of time;
3. when the Commodity Futures Trading Commission denies, suspends, or revokes registration;
4. when a foreign financial regulatory authority denies, suspends, or revokes the person's authority to conduct transactions;
5. when conduct has been found to be a cause of any effective suspension or order by a domestic or foreign exchange or authority;
6. when a person has associated himself with another who is subject to a statutory disqualification and it was known or should have been known.

MSRB RULE G-37

Political contributions and prohibitions on municipal securities business (MSRB Rule G-37) - the Rule is intended to ensure high standards of integrity in the municipal securities industry. It prohibits brokers, dealers, and municipal securities dealer from engaging in business with issuers if certain political contributions have been made to officials of such issuers. It also requires brokers, dealers, and municipal securities dealers to disclose certain political contributions and other information.

SECTION 202(A)(11)

Definitions of investment adviser (Section 202(a)(11)) - a person who advises others regarding the value of securities and the advisability of investing, for compensation and promulgates analyses and reports on a regular basis. The definition does not include certain banks, lawyers, accountants, engineers, teachers, broker-dealers whose performance of services is incidental to the practice of his profession, publishers of bona fide news, certain persons who advise regarding obligations of the United States, recognized statistical rating organizations, or certain family offices.

SEC RULE 17A-3

Subsidiary ledgers and proofs of money balances in all accounts - in the form of trial balances, and a record of the computation of aggregate indebtedness and net capital.

Questionnaire or application for employment executed by each associated person - approved in writing by an authorized representative of the broker or dealer, and is to include specific identifying and professional information for such person.

Fingerprint records required by Rule 17f-2 - every member of a national securities exchange, broker, dealer, registered transfer agent and registered clearing agency is to maintain the fingerprint card along with any other information received by the Attorney General, for every person required to be fingerprinted.

RULE 17F-2

Fingerprinting of securities industry personnel (Rule 17f-2) - any member of a national securities exchange, broker, dealer, registered transfer agent or registered clearing agency must require each of its partners, directors, officers, and employees be fingerprinted and submit the fingerprints to the Attorney General of the United States, with some exemptions.

REGISTRATION OF INVESTMENT ADVISERS

Investment advisers must be registered with the SEC unless they meet certain specific criteria for an exemption. In order to register the adviser is to submit an application to the SEC with specific information. The SEC will, within 45 days, either grant registration or begin proceeding to determine if it is to be denied. The SEC reserves the right to suspend or revoke the registration at any time for cause. An adviser may be exempt from the registration requirement if:

1. he is an adviser whose clients reside in the same state in which the adviser maintains his business and who does advise on securities listed on a national securities exchange;
2. his only clients are insurance companies;
3. he is a foreign private adviser;
4. he is a charitable organization;
5. it is a plan described in Section 414(e) of the IRS code, or he is a person who advises solely regarding entities that are excluded from the definition of an investment company;
6. he is one of certain advisers registered with the Commodity Futures Trading Commission;
7. he is one of certain advisers who advise solely regarding certain small business investment companies.

SECTION 205

Investment advisory contracts (Section 205) - investment advisory contracts may not provide an investment adviser a compensation based on a share of capital gains or capital appreciation of a client's funds; may not fail to provide that no assignment of the contract can be made by the adviser without consent of the other party; and may not fail to provide that, if adviser is a partnership, the adviser will notify the party of any change in membership of partnership.

SECTION 206

Prohibited transactions by investment advisers (Section 206) - it is unlawful for any investment adviser:

1. to employ any device, scheme, or artifice to defraud a client
2. to engage in any course of business that operates as a fraud or deceit
3. acting in his own account, to sell or purchase any security to or from a client without disclosing to the client in writing before the completion of the sale
4. to engage in any business practice that is fraudulent, deceptive, or manipulative

TERMS IN ARTICLE 1 OF FINRA BY-LAWS

Found in Article 1 of the FINRA By-Laws:

Act — Securities Exchange Act of 1934.

Board — the Board of Governors of the Corporation.

Closing — the closing of the consolidation of certain member firm regulatory functions of NYSE Regulation, Inc. and the Corporation.

Commission — the Securities and Exchange Commission.

Corporation — National Association of Securities Dealers, Inc. or any future name of the entity.

Delegation plan — the Plan of Allocation and Delegation of Functions by NASD to Subsidiaries.

District — a district established by the NASD Regulation Board.

Floor member governor — a member of the Board who is associated with a member specialist or floor broker on the NYSE trading floor.

Governor — member of the Board.

Independent dealer/insurance affiliate governor — a member of the board associated with a member who is an independent contractor financial planning member firm or insurance company.

Industry director — a director of the NASD Regulation Board who has served in the previous year as on officer or has a consulting employment relationship with a self regulatory organization.

Industry governor — the floor member governor, independent dealer/insurance affiliate governor, and investment company affiliate governor and any other governor who has served in the previous year as an officer, or has a consulting employment relationship with a self regulatory organization.

Investment company affiliate governor — member of the Board associated with an investment company member.

Joint public governor — the public governor to be appointed by the Board of Directors of the NYSE Group, Inc. and the Board in office prior to the closing jointly.

Large firm — a broker/dealer member with 500 or more registered persons.

Large firm governor — a member of the board to be elected by large firm members.

Large firm governor committee — a committee of the Board comprised of all the large firm governors.

Lead governor — a member of the Board elected as such.

Mid-size firm — any broker/dealer member with at least 151, and no more than 499, registered persons.

Mid-size firm governor — a member of the board elected by mid-size firm members.

Member — any broker/dealer admitted to membership in the Corporation.

NASD group committee — a committee of the Board comprised of the five public governors, the independent dealer/insurance affiliate governor, and the small firm governors.

NASD public governors — the five public governors appointed as such.

NYSE group committee — a committee of the Board comprised of the five public governors, the floor member governor, and the large firm governors nominated by the NYSE Group Inc.

NYSE public governors — the five public governors appointed by the Board of Directors of NYSE Group, Inc.

Public director — a director of the NASD Regulation Board.

Public governor — a governor or committee member who is not the CEO of the Corporation.

Small firm — and broker/dealer member with 1 to 150 registered persons.

Small firm governor — a member of the Board elected by small firm members.

Small firm governor committee — a committee of the Board comprised of all the small firm governors.

ARTICLE 3 OF FINRA BY-LAWS
SECTION 1

According to Section 1 of Article 3 of the FINRA By-Laws:

Persons eligible to become members and associated persons of members (Section 1) - any registered broker, dealer, municipal securities broker or dealer, or government securities broker or dealer can be members. Any person can be an associated person of a member, unless otherwise ineligible.

Authority of Board to adopt qualification requirements (Section 2) - the Board has the authority to adopt rules and regulations applicable to applicants.

Definition of disqualification (Section 4) - a person is disqualified in regards to membership if the person is subject to a statutory disqualification.

SECTION 3

As found in Section 3 of Article 3 of the FINRA By-Laws:

Ineligibility of certain persons for membership or association (Section 3) - no registered broker, dealer, municipal securities broker or dealer, or government securities broker or dealer can be a member if he fails to satisfy the qualification requirements. No person can be associated with a member if the person does not meet the qualification requirements. The Board has the authority to cancel a person's membership. If a member is found to be ineligible, the member can file an application for relief with the Board.

ARTICLE 5 OF THE FINRA BY-LAWS

Article 5 of the FINRA By-Laws discusses registered representatives and associated persons:

Qualification requirements (Section 1) - a member is not to permit an associated person to engage in investment banking or securities business unless such person meets the qualification requirements.

Application for registration (Section 2) - a signed application for membership is to be submitted electronically and is to contain:

1. an agreement to comply with governing laws, rules, and regulations;
2. other reasonable information required by the Corporation.

Notification by member to the Corporation and associated person of termination; amendments to notification (Section 3) - if a member terminates an associated person, the member is to give notice to the Corporation within 30 days, and give a copy of the same notice to the person terminated. If the member finds any facts in such notice to be incomplete or inaccurate, the member is to file an amendment and submit it to the Corporation with a copy to the person terminated within 30 days of first learning of the facts.

Retention of jurisdiction (Section 4) - a person who has had his association with a member terminated is still subject to filing a complaint based upon conduct that began prior to termination.

NASD RULE 1010

An applicant for membership is to file an application according to Rule 1013. An applicant seeking approval of change in ownership, control, or business operations is to file an application according to Rule 1017. Unless FINRA has prescribed an electronic or other filing process, an applicant can file by first-class mail, overnight courier, or hand delivery. A facsimile is acceptable if the applicant and FINRA agree. FINRA may serve a notice or decision by first-class mail. Service by FINRA or filing by an applicant is complete:

1. as of the postmarked date for first-class mail;
2. as of the date of delivery for overnight courier;
3. on the date of receipt for hand delivery;
4. upon written confirmation of transmission and the date specified in the document for facsimile; and
5. upon the date of confirmation for electronic filing

LAPSE OF APPLICATION

A lapse occurs when an applicant does not respond fully within 60 days after being served with an initial request for information, when the applicant does not appear or participate in a schedule membership interview, or when the applicant does not file an executed membership agreement within 25 days after service of the agreement.

A new member application is to include - Form NMA; an original, signed, and notarized Form BD; a FINRA approved fingerprint card; a new member assessment report; a detailed business plan; a copy of any court decisions that take adverse action in regards to registration or licensing; a list of all associated persons; documentation of specific events; a description of any remedial action; a written acknowledgement that heightened supervisory procedures and special education programs may be required; a copy of contract with banks, clearing entities, or service bureaus; a description of the nature and source of capital; a description of financial controls; a description of the supervisory system, including copies of procedures; a description of the number, experience, and qualifications of supervisors; a description of the proposed record-keeping system; a copy of the written training plan to comply with firm element continuing education requirements; and a FINRA Entitlement Program Agreement and Terms of Use as well as a FINRA Member Firm Account Administrator Entitlement Form.

When the FINRA Member Firm Account Administrator Entitlement Form is approved - the member is to submit a Form U4 for every associated person. If the Department needs additional information, the applicant is to comply with its requests within 60 days of receiving the original request. If an applicant withdraws his application within 30 days after filing, FINRA will refund the application fee, except for $500 kept as a processing fee.

Membership Interview - the Department is to have a membership interview with a representative of the applicant before making a decision. Such interview is to occur within 90 days after the filing of the application and will happen in the district office where the applicant has its principal place of business.

Department decision - after considering the application, interview, and any other information, the Department will make a decision on whether or not the applicant meets the standards for membership. The Department can either grant the membership, deny the application, or grant the applicant membership subject to specific restrictions. This decision is to be made within 30 days after completion of the interview or filing of additional documents.

Review by the National Adjudicatory Council - if an applicant believes a decision to be inconsistent with membership standards, he can request a review with the National Adjudicatory Council. Upon receipt of such request, FINRA will, within ten days, transmit it with any pertinent documentation to the Council. The Council will appoint a subcommittee to review the request, and it may request a hearing. In the end, the Council can affirm, modify, or reverse the Department's decision.

Discretionary review by FINRA Board - a governor has the ability to call for a review of a membership proceeding, and such review is to happen at the next meeting. FINRA may then affirm, modify, or reverse the proposed written decision.

Application for approval of change in ownership, control or business operations - a member is to file an application in the case of certain mergers, acquisitions, changes of equity ownership, and material changes in business operations.

Application to Commission for review - a person aggrieved by a final action under FINRA Rule 1010 can apply for review to the Securities Exchange Commission.

Terms found in NASD Rule 1010:

Department — the Department of Member Regulation of FINRA.

Director — a member of the FINRA Regulation Board.

FINRA Board — the Board of Governors of FINRA.

FINRA Regulation Board — the Board of Directors of FINRA Regulation.

Governor — a member of the FINRA Board.

Interested FINRA Staff — an employee who participates in a decision.

Sales practice event — any customer complaint, arbitration, or civil litigation that has been reported.

FINRA Rule 1010

The enumerated uniform forms are to be filed electronically. A member is to identify a registered principal with authority over registration functions to be responsible for the supervision of the electronic filing of forms. The electronic filing of a Form U4 is to be based on a manually signed Form U4 by the person on whose behalf the form is being filed, though amendments to the Form can be filed electronically without a manually signed form needed. Fingerprint information is to be sent to FINRA within 30 days of the Form U4 filing, or the registration will be deemed inactive. Initial filing and amendments of Form U5 are to be filed electronically.

FINRA Rule 1122 and NASD Rule 1000

Filing of misleading information as to membership or registration (FINRA Rule 1122) - a member may not file information with FINRA having to do with membership or registration that is incomplete or accurate so as to be misleading. If a member does so, it is to be immediately corrected.

Failure to register personnel (NASD IM-1000-3) - if a member fails to register an employee as a registered representative who should be so registered it is found to be conduct inconsistent with just and equitable principles of trade, and may be cause for disciplinary action.

Branch offices and offices of supervisory jurisdiction (NASD IM-1000-4) - a member is required to ensure that its membership application is kept current by means of supplementary amendments and to ensure that the main office is properly designated and registered, if required. A member is required to designate offices of supervisory jurisdiction, and must register those branch offices.

CONTINUING EDUCATION REQUIREMENTS FOR MEMBERSHIP AND REGISTRATION
REGULATORY ELEMENT

Members are to meet the continuing education requirements, their regulatory element, on their 2nd registration anniversary and every three years thereafter. If it is not completed, the person's registration will be deemed inactive. A registered person is required to retake the regulatory element and satisfy all the requirements if the person is subject to a statutory disqualification, is subject to a suspension, or is ordered to as part of a sanction. If FINRA procedures are followed, a firm can have an "in-firm" administration of the regulatory requirement for their registered persons.

FIRM ELEMENT

A member firm must maintain a continuing and current education program for its covered registered persons to enhance the securities skills, knowledge, and professionalism. Annually, a member is to evaluate and prioritize his training needs and develop a plan.

FINRA RULES 3220 AND 2263

Influencing or rewarding employees of others (FINRA Rule 3220) - a member is not to give anything of value in excess of $100 per individual per person per year in relation to the business of the employer.

Arbitration disclosure to associated persons signing or acknowledging Form U4 (FINRA Rule 2263) - a member is to provide an associated person with a specific written statement at any time the person is asked to sign or initial a Form U4. This statement ensures the person understands predispute arbitration.

RULE 9500 OF THE FINRA CODE OF PROCEDURES
ELIGIBILITY PROCEEDINGS

If FINRA believes a member or person associated with a member does not met eligibility requirements, FINRA will sent him a notice of such. The notice states that the recipient can apply for relief. The Department of Member Regulation is authorized to grant relief from the eligibility requirements under certain circumstances.

EXPEDITED PROCEEDINGS

The following issues will be processed in an expedited manner: failure to comply with public communication standards; failure to provide information or keep information current; failure to pay FINRA dues, fees and other charges; failure to comply with an arbitration award or related settlement or an order of restitution or settlement providing for restitution; failure to meet the eligibility or qualification standards or prerequisites for access to services; failure to comply with temporary and permanent cease and desist orders; procedures for regulating activities under Rules 4110, 4120, and 4130 regarding a member experiencing financial or operational difficulties; summary proceedings for actions authorized by Section 15A(h)(3) of the Exchange Act; and hearing procedures for expedited proceedings under the Rule 9550 series.

NASD RULE 1020

Registration requirements found in NASD Rule 1020 are explained below.

PRINCIPALS

All persons engaged as principals in the investment banking or securities business of a member must be registered with NASD. In order to be registered, they must pass a Qualification Examination according to their category of registration. A principal is defined as a person actively engaged in investment banking or securities business, which includes supervision, solicitation, conduct of business, or training of persons for the same functions. Principals include sole proprietors, officers, partners, managers of offices of supervisory jurisdiction, and directors of corporations. If a registration has lapsed for two or more years, the person will be required to take a Qualification Examination again for his category of registration.

GENERAL SECURITIES PRINCIPAL

A person associated with a member as either a principal or a Chief Compliance Officer must be registered as a General Securities Principal. A person seeking to be registered as a General Securities Principal must first be registered as a General Securities Representative or a Limited Representative - Corporate Securities, or if such person is to have a supervisory role, he must be first registered as a Limited Representative - Investment Banking.

LIMITED PRINCIPAL

Financial and Operations: Every member is to appoint at least one Limited Principal - Financial Operations, which is to be the chief financial officer. This person's duties include final approval for accuracy of financial reports; final preparation of financial reports; supervision of preparation of financial reports; supervision of and responsibility for those involved in maintenance of books and records; supervision of and responsibility for those involved in administration of back office operations; or any other matter involving financial and operational management.

Introducing Broker/Dealer Financial and Operations: Every member is to appoint at least one Limited Principal - Introducing Broker/Dealer, which is to be the chief financial officer. This person's duties include final approval for accuracy of financial reports; final preparation of financial reports; supervision of preparation of financial reports; supervision of and responsibility for those involved in maintenance of books and records; supervision of the member's responsibilities under the financial responsibility rules pursuant to provisions of the Act; and supervision of and responsibility for those involved in administration of back office operations; or any other matter involving financial and operational management.

Investment Company and Variable Contracts Products: A person associated with a member may register as a Limited Principal - Investment Company and Variable Contracts Products if the person is already registered as a General Securities Representative or Limited Representative - Investment Company and Variable Contracts Products; if the person passes the corresponding Qualification Examination; and if the person's duties are limited to solicitation, purchase, or sale of certain investment companies' redeemable securities, certain closed-end investment companies' securities, and certain exempt variable contracts and insurance premium funding programs.

Direct Participation Programs: A person associated with a member may register as a Limited Principal - Direct Participation Programs if the person is already registered as a General Securities Representative or a Limited Representative - Direct Participation Programs; if the person passes the corresponding Qualification Examination; and if the person's duties are limited to the equity interests in or the debt of direct participation programs.

Registered Options and Security Future: Every member engaged in the business of futures and options is to have at least one Registered Options and Security Futures Principal, and all persons engaged in the supervision of options and security futures sales practices is to be registered as such. This person must pass the corresponding Qualification Examination; and must already be registered as a General Securities Representative or a Limited Representative - Corporate Securities and a Registered Options and Security Futures Representative.

General Securities Sales Supervisor: A person associated with a member may register as a Limited Principal - General Securities Sales Supervisor if the person has passed a corresponding examination; has already been registered as a General Securities Representative; and if the person's supervisory responsibilities are limited to securities sales activities.

Government Securities: A person associated with a member who has not previously registered as a principal and is to work as a government securities principal is to register as such. A person must be registered as a Limited Principal - Government Securities if they are engaged in the management of the member's government securities business which includes the following activities relating to government securities: underwriting, trading, sales, financial advisory, research or investment advice, communication with public investors, supervision of processing and clearance activities, and supervision of the maintenance of records.

NASD RULE 1030

Registration requirements (NASD Rule 1031) - any person engaged as a representative in the investment banking or securities business of a member must be registered. In order to be registered, he must pass a Qualification Examination according to their category of registration. A representative is defined as a person associated with a member including assistant officers other than principals, involved in the investment banking or securities business including functions such as supervision, solicitation, and training. If a person's registration has lapsed for two or more years, the person is required to retake a Qualification Examination for Representatives corresponding to his registration.

NASD RULE 1032

GENERAL SECURITIES REPRESENTATIVE

Any representative associated with a member is required to register as a General Securities Representative, unless his activities are limited enough to qualify him for one of the limited categories of representation.

LIMITED REPRESENTATIVE

Investment Company and Variable Contracts Products: A representative associated with a member may register as a Limited Representative - Investment Company and Variable Contracts Products if his activities are limited to the solicitation, purchase, or sale of certain investment companies' redeemable securities, certain closed-end investment companies' securities, and certain exempt variable contracts and insurance premium funding programs, and the person passes a corresponding Qualification Examination.

Direct Participation Program: A representative associated with a member may register as a Limited Representative - Direct Participation Program if his activities are limited to the equity interests in or the debt of direct participation programs, and the person passes a corresponding Qualification Examination. A person seeking this registration must already have been registered as a Limited Representative - Corporate Securities or Limited Representative - Government Securities.

Options and Security Futures: A representative associated with a member may register as a Limited Representative - Direct Participation Program if his activities involve solicitation or sale of option or security futures contracts, and the person passes a corresponding Qualification Examination.

Corporate Securities: A representative associated with a member may register as a Limited Representative - Corporate Securities if he has passed a corresponding Qualification Examination and his activities involve the solicitation, purchase, or sale of securities other than municipal securities, option securities, redeemable securities, variable contracts of certain insurance companies, and direct participation programs.

Equity Trader: Every representative associated with a member must register as a Limited Representative - Equity Trader if in regards to equity securities he engages in proprietary trading, transacting on an agency basis, or supervises such activities. A person seeking this registration must have already been registered as a General Securities Representative or a Limited Representative - Corporate Securities and the person must pass a corresponding Qualification Examination.

Government Securities: A representative associated with a member may register as a Limited Representative - Government Securities if the person's activities involve the solicitation, purchase, or sale of government securities and the person passes a corresponding Qualification Examination.

Private Securities Offerings: A representative associated with a member may register as a Limited Representative - Private Securities Offerings if his activities involve effecting sales as part of certain primary non-public offerings but not the sales of municipal, government, or equity interest or debt of direct participation programs. Such person also must pass a corresponding Qualification Examination.

Investment Banking: A representative associated with a member must register as a Limited Representative - Investment Banking if his activities involve advising on debt or equity securities or advising on or facilitating mergers and acquisitions, tender offers, financial restructurings, asset sales, divestitures or other corporate reorganizations, unless such person's activities are limited to advising on the placement of direct participation program securities, private securities offerings, or retail or institutional sales activities. He also must pass a corresponding Qualification Examination.

NASD RULES 1041 AND 1042

Registration requirements for assistant representatives (NASD Rule 1041) - an Assistant Representative - Order Processing of a member must be registered. He must pass a corresponding Qualification Examination.

Restrictions for assistant representatives (NASD Rule 1042) - an Assistant Representative - Order Processing is not to solicit any transactions or new accounts, give investment advice or recommendations, or make transactions in securities. He may only be compensated an hourly or salary basis, and not in relation to the number or size of transactions.

NASD RULES 1050 AND 1060

Registration of research analysts (NASD Rule 1050) - all research analysts associated with a member are to be registered. The analysts must first be registered as a General Securities Representative and have passed a Qualification Examination.

Persons exempt from registration (NASD Rule 1060) - certain persons associated with a member are exempt from registration including: clerical or ministerial persons; persons not actively engaged in investment banking or securities business; persons that are nominal officers or capital participants; certain persons registered on the floor of a national securities exchange; and persons engaged in only municipal securities, commodities, or security futures. Compensation can be given to certain non-registered foreign-associated persons.

NASD Rules 1070 and 1080

Qualification examinations and waiver of requirements (NASD Rule 1070) - Qualification Examinations are a series of questions based on topic outlines from the Association. Results from such examinations are given to the member firms. In certain cases, NASD may waive the requirement of a Qualification Examination in lieu of other standard acceptable as proof of qualification. If a person fails the examination, he may take it again after 30 days, unless he has failed three times, in which case he must wait a period of 180 days.

Confidentiality of examinations (NASD Rule 1080) - the Qualification Examinations are confidential. An exam is not to be removed from the examination center, and any reproduction, disclosure, or receipt of any portion of the exam is prohibited.

NASD Rule 1100

Foreign associates (NASD Rule 1100) - foreign persons associated with a member must register but are not required to pass a Qualification Examination, as long as they meet the following criteria:

1. they are not citizens, nationals, or residents of the United States; and
2. all their activities will be conducted outside of the United States and not with any citizen, national, or resident of the United States.

The member must file a Uniform Application for Securities Industry Registration or Transfer for the person to make certifications that the criteria have been met.

NASD Rule 3010
Supervisory System

Every members is to have a supervisory system in place to ensure compliance with laws, regulations, and rules. The system is to have, at minimum, the following:

1. written procedures
2. designation of registered principals with the authority to carry out supervisory responsibilities
3. designation as an office of supervisory jurisdiction (OSJ) in each required location
4. designation of registered principals in each OSJ with the authority to carry out supervisory responsibilities of that office
5. assignment of each registered person to a registered representative responsible for supervising that person's activities
6. reasonable efforts to determine that all supervisors are qualified in experience or training
7. participation of each registered representative and registered principal in an annual meeting to discuss compliance of supervisory activities

Written Procedures

Every member is to establish, maintain, and enforce written procedures to supervise the types of business it is engaged in, as well as to supervise the registered representatives and principals designated to achieve compliance.

Tape recording of conversations - certain firms may be required to tape record any telemarketing activities of their registered persons speaking with customers or potential customers. If NASD informs the member that it is subject to the tape recording of telemarketing activities, the member firm has 60 days to establish and implement the supervisory procedures involved. Any such recording are to be kept for at least three years.

Required information in written procedures - the titles, registration status, and locations of the supervisory personnel as well as the responsibilities of each.

Location - a copy of the written procedures are to be kept in each office of supervisory jurisdiction.

INTERNAL INSPECTIONS

Annually, a member is to review its business to detect and prevent violations of applicable securities laws, regulations, and rules. The member is to review each of its offices, and examine periodically customer accounts to detect irregularities or abuses. The review is not to be conducted by the office manager or person with supervisory responsibilities in that same office. There is to be a written report of such review that is to be kept for at least three years, and is to contain the testing and verification of policies and procedures in the following areas:

1. safeguarding of customer funds and securities
2. maintaining books and records
3. supervision of customer accounts
4. transmission of funds
5. validation of customer address changes
6. validation of changes in customer account information

REVIEW OF TRANSACTIONS AND CORRESPONDENCE

Supervision of registered representatives - a member is to establish procedures for the review and endorsement of a registered principal for all transactions, and for the review of a registered principal of all incoming and outgoing electronic correspondence with the public regarding investment banking or securities business.

Review of correspondence - a member is to develop written procedures for the review of incoming and outgoing correspondence with the public regarding investment banking and securities business in order to properly identify and handle customer complaints and to ensure compliance with procedures.

Retention of correspondence - correspondence regarding investment banking or securities business is to be retained. The names of the persons who prepared outgoing correspondence and who reviewed the correspondence are to be easily ascertainable.

QUALIFICATIONS INVESTIGATED AND APPLICANT'S RESPONSIBILITY

Qualifications investigated - a member is responsible for the investigation of the good character, business repute, qualifications, and experience of any person prior to certifying such in the application to the NASD.

Applicant's responsibility - if an applicant has before been registered and the applicant's Form U-5 (Uniform Termination Notice of Securities Industry Registration) is being requested in regards to his previous employer, the member is to provide a copy within two business days.

SUPERVISORY JURISDICTION AND BRANCH OFFICE

Office of supervisory jurisdiction (OSJ) - any office of a member where 1 of the following functions takes place: order execution and/or market making; structuring of public offering/private placements; maintaining custody of customer's funds or securities; final acceptance of new accounts; review and endorsement of customer orders; final approval of retail communications; or responsibility for supervising activities.

Branch office - any location where one or more associated persons regularly conduct the business of effecting transactions or inducing the purchase or sale of any security, except for exclusively customer service or back office functions, or private residences.

STANDARDS FOR REASONABLE REVIEW

Standards for reasonable review (IM 3010-1) - a member is to conduct annually a review of its business to detect and prevent violations of and achieve compliance with laws, regulations, and rules. Each review must take into consideration the member's size, organizational structure, scope of business activities, number and location of offices, the nature and complexity of products and services offered, the volume of business, the number of associated persons assigned to a location, whether a location has a principal on-site, whether the office is a non-branch location, and the disciplinary history of the registered representatives or associated persons.

CRD, BROKERCHECK HOTLINE, EXECUTIVE REPRESENTATIVES

FINRA/NASAA Central Registration Depository - The CRD is the main licensing and registrations system in the United States for the securities industry. In it is information on a large number of broker-dealers, including registration information, disclosure information, and qualification information on their associated persons.

FINRA has instated the BrokerCheck Hotline for the purposes of providing a resource for those seeking information regarding a specific broker, including public disciplinary information.

Executive representative - As found in NASD Rule 1150, each member is to identify, review, and update its executive representative and contact information.

Supervision of General Broker-Dealer Activities

FINRA Rule 3130

Annual certification of compliance and supervisory processes - every member is to designate one or more principals to serve as chief compliance officer (CCO). The CCO is to certify annually that the member has processes in place to establish, maintain, review, test, and modify compliance policies and procedures designed to achieve compliance.

FINRA Rule 4370

Every member is to create and maintain a business continuity plan with procedures relating to an emergency or significant business disruption. These procedures are to be designed as to enable the member to continue to meet obligations to customers. The plan is to be updated in relation to any material change in operations, structure, business, or location. The plan is to be reviewed annually. The member must disclose to its customers how the plan addresses significant business disruption. The member is to submit to FINRA emergency contact information. At a minimum, the plan must address:

1. data back-up and recovery
2. all mission critical systems
3. financial and operational assessments
4. alternate communications between customers and the member
5. alternate communications between the member and its employees
6. alternate physical location of employees
7. critical business constituent, bank, and counter-party impact
8. regulatory reporting
9. communications with regulators
10. how the member will assure customers' prompt access to their funds if the member can no longer do business

FINRA Rules 8110 and 8210

Availability of manual to customers (FINRA Rule 8110) - a member is to make a current copy of the FINRA Manual available to customers upon their request.

Provision of information and testimony and inspection and copying of books (FINRA Rule 8210) - an Adjudicator on FINRA staff has the right to require a member or associated person to provide information and to testify. He also has the right to inspect books and records. FINRA may, under an agreement with another regulatory organization, share information for regulatory purposes.

NASD Rule 3012
SUPERVISORY CONTROL SYSTEM

Supervisory control system - each member is to identify one or more principles who will establish, maintain, and enforce a system of supervisory control policies and procedures that test and verify that the supervisory procedures are reasonably designed to achieve compliance, and create additional supervisory procedures when the need is identified. These written supervisory control policies and procedures are to include:

1. procedures designed to review and supervise customer account activity;
2. procedures designed to review and supervise all transmission of funds, customer changes of address, and customer changes of investment activities;
3. and procedures designed to provide heightened supervision over activities of producing managers responsible for 20% or more of the revenue of a business unit.

SEC RULE 15C1-8 AND FINRA RULE 2060

Sales at the market (SEC Rule 15c1-8) - a broker cannot sell a security in which the broker is financially interested and not found on a national exchange to a customer "at the market" price unless the broker has a reasonable belief that a market for the security exists outside of the market that he controls.

Use of information obtained in a fiduciary capacity (FINRA Rule 2060) - no member can use information regarding ownership of securities to sell securities.

FINRA RULE 2150

Improper Use - no person associated with a member is to make improper use of a customer's securities or funds.

Prohibition against guarantees - no member or associated person is to guarantee a customer against loss regarding any securities transactions or in any account.

Sharing in accounts; Extent permissible - no member or person associated is to share in the profits or losses of a customer's account, unless

1. there is prior written authorization from the member;
2. there is prior written authorization from the customer; and
3. the sharing of profit or loss is directly proportionate to the amount contributed to the account by the member or person associated.

FINRA RULE 2320

Application - the Rule applies to members in connection with variable contracts.

Definition of purchase payment - consideration paid at each purchase or installment for the variable contract.

Definition of variable contact - a contact providing benefits or value that may vary according to investment experience of the separate accounts of an insurance company.

Receipt of payment - a member is not to offer or sell a variable contract other than on the basis of a value determined following receipt or payment in accordance with the contract.

Transmittal - a member is to transmit promptly to the issuer, all applications and appropriate amounts of the purchase payments received.

Selling agreements - a member who is a principal underwriter may not sell variable contracts through another broker-dealer unless such broker-dealer is a member and there is a sales agreement in place.

Redemption - a member may not sell a variable contract of an insurance company unless such company makes prompt redemption payments of requested amounts payable under the contract.

FINRA Rule 3240

Permissible lending arrangements; conditions - a person associated with a member is not to borrow money from or lend money to a customer unless the member has written procedures allowing it or the arrangement meets one of the following conditions:

1. the customer is part of the person's immediate family;
2. the customer is a certain type of financial institution;
3. the customer and the person are both registered persons of the same member;
4. the arrangement is based on a personal relationship with the customer; or
5. the arrangement is based on a business relationship outside of the broker-customer relationship.

Notification and approval - the member is to be notified of such arrangements and must give written approval, unless otherwise stated in the member's policies.

Definition of immediate family - includes parents, grandparents, mother and father-in-law, husband or wife, brother or sister, brother or sister-in-law, son or daughter-in-law, children, grandchildren, cousin, aunt or uncle, niece or nephew, and any other person that the person supports.

Record Retention (Supplementary Material - .01) - the written approval is to be kept for at least three years.

FINRA Rule 3270

A registered person cannot work for an outside person, or be compensated in any way from an outside person without the prior written consent of the member firm in regards to business activity outside the scope of the relationship with the member firm.

NASD Rule 3040

Applicability - the Rule is applicable to all persons associated with a member.

Written notice - before participating in a private securities transaction, a person associated with a member is to provide written notice to the member.

Transactions for compensation - if a person associated with a member participates in such a transaction for compensation, the person is to submit the written notice and the member can approve or disapprove of such transaction. If approved, the transaction is entered into the books of the member. If disapproved, the person cannot participate.

Transactions not for compensation - if a person associated with a member participates in such a transaction and no compensation is involved, the written notice must still be given and the member may require certain conditions.

Definition of private securities transaction - a securities transaction outside the person's regular course of employment with a member that is not registered with the Commission.

Definition of selling compensation - any compensation received in connection with the purchase or sale of a security.

NASD Rule 3050

Determine adverse interest - a member who knowingly executes a transaction to purchase or sell a security for the account of person associated with another member is to use due diligence in ensuring that the transaction will not adversely affect the persons employing member.

Obligations of executing member - the executing member is to notify the employing member in writing prior to execution; to transmit copies of confirmations, statements, or other information upon request; and to notify the person associated of the intent to provide such information.

Obligations of associated persons concerning an account with a member - the person associated in such a transaction is to notify both the executing member and employing member of his association with each.

Obligations of associated persons concerning an account with an investment adviser, bank, or other financial institution - if a person associated with a member opens a securities account or places an order for the purchase or sale of a security with a notice-registered broker or dealer, investment advisor, bank, or other financial institution that is not a member, the person is to notify his employing member in writing and, upon the written request of the employing member, request in writing that the financial institution provides the employing member with copies of confirmations, statements, or other financial information.

Exemption for transactions in investment company shares and unit investment trusts - the Rule is not applicable to transactions in certain unit investment trusts and variable contracts or redeemable securities.

Sections 9(a)(1) and 9(a)(2) of SEA

Misleading appearance of active trading (Section 9(a)(1)) - it is prohibited for any person to do any of the following for the purposes of creating a false or misleading appearance of active trading in a security other than a government security:

1. make a transaction that involves no change of ownership;
2. enter purchase orders for a security knowing that substantially the same order of the same size, time, and price will be entered as well;
3. enter sell orders for a security knowing that substantially the same order of the same size, time, and price will be entered as well.

Inducing purchase or sale by others (Section 9(a)(2)) - it is prohibited for any person to, for the purposes of inducing the purchase or sale of a security by others, make a series of transactions in a security other than a government security to create actual or apparent active trading, or raising and lowering the price of the security.

Sections 9(a)(3) and 9(a)(4) of SEA

Dissemination of information as to rise or fall of security prices (Section 9(a)(3)) - it is prohibited for any person to, for the purposes of raising or depressing the price of a security, to induce the purchase or sale of a security other than a government security by the circulation or dissemination of information suggesting that the price will rise or fall because of market conditions.

Making false or misleading statements (Section 9(a)(4)) - it is prohibited for any person, for the purpose of inducing the purchase or sale of a security, to make a statement that is false or misleading regarding a material fact when the person has reasonable grounds to believe the statement was false or misleading.

Sections 9(a)(5) and 9(a)(6) of SEA

Dissemination of information for consideration (Section 9(a)(5)) - it is prohibited for any person, for the purpose of raising or lowering the price of a security, to induce the purchase of a security other than a government security by the circulation or dissemination of information suggesting that the price will rise or fall because of market conditions for a consideration.

Pegging, fixing, or stabilizing prices (Section 9(a)(6)) - it is prohibited for any person to, for the purposes of pegging, fixing, or stabilizing the price, make a series of transactions for the purchase and/or sale of a security other than a government security.

Section 9(f)

Liability for unlawful acts or transactions (Section 9(f)) - a person who willfully participates in transactions prohibited in Section 9 of the Securities Exchange Act of 1934 is liable to any person who purchases or sells any security at a price affected by the prohibited act. The injured person may sue to recover damages sustained as well as legal costs. Any actions enforcing liability as found in this section must be made within one year after the discovery of the facts constituting violation and within three years of the violation itself.

SEA Rules 10b-1 and 10b5-2

Prohibitions with respect to securities exempted from registration (Rule 10b-1) - it is prohibited to use any manipulative or deceptive device in connection with securities exempt from registration pursuant to the SEA.

Duties of trust or confidence in misappropriation insider trading cases (Rule 10b5-2) - a duty of trust and confidence exists:

1. when a person agrees to maintain information in confidence
2. when the persons involved in communicating the material nonpublic information have a history or practice of sharing confidences to the extent that the communicator trusts the information will remain confidential
3. or when a person receives information from a spouse, parent, child, or sibling

SEA Rules 10b-3 and 10b-5

Employment of manipulative and deceptive devices by brokers or dealers (Rule 10b-3) - it is prohibited for a broker or dealer to purchase or sell a security otherwise than on a national exchange with an act that is manipulative, deceptive, or fraudulent. The same is also prohibited for municipal securities dealers and municipal securities.

Employment of manipulative and deceptive devices (Rule 10b-5) - it is prohibited for any person to employ and device, scheme, or artifice to defraud; to make any untrue statements of material fact; or to engage in any act, practice, or course of business that would be a fraud or deceit upon any person in connections with the purchase or sale of any security.

SEA Rule 10b-17

Untimely announcements of record dates (Rule 10b-17) - an issuer must, in relation to a dividend, stock split, reverse stock split, or a rights offering, give notice to the National Association of Securities Dealers, Inc. (NASD) before ten days prior to the record date. The notice is to include the title of the security to which the declaration relates, date of declaration, date of record, date of payment, method of settlement of fractional interests, details of any condition that must be satisfied to enable payment, and, if a stock split or reverse split, the name and address of the transfer agent.

SEC RULE 10B-18

Purchases of certain equity securities by the issuer and others (Rule 10b-18) - a purchase has not violated anti-manipulation provisions of the Securities Exchange Act of 1934 if the issuer or affiliated purchaser makes the transactions according to each of the following conditions:

1. the purchase is made by one broker-dealer on a single day
2. Time of purchases:
   a. the purchase is not the opening purchase reported in the consolidated system
   b. the purchase is not made during the ten minutes before close of the trading session in the principal market of the security, for certain securities that have an average daily trade volume of $1 million or more
   c. the purchase is not made during the 30 minutes before close of the trading session in the principal market of the security, for all other securities
   d. However, purchases can be made in certain instances after the close of primary trading session so long as the purchases meet certain price criteria

Price of purchases:

1. the purchase is not to exceed the highest independent bid
2. for securities not in the consolidated system, the purchase does not exceed the highest independent bid displayed on any national securities exchange or inter-dealer quotation system
3. for all other securities, purchases must be made at a price that is not higher than the highest independent bid from three independent dealers

Volume of purchases - the total volume of a security traded in a single day is not to exceed 25% of the average daily trade volume.

Alternative conditions - the rule applies to purchases made in a session following a market-wide trade suspension, except the time of purchases conditions do not apply, and the volume of purchases condition is modified to a limit of 100% of average daily trade volume.

SECTION 15 OF THE SEA
SECTION 15(A)(1) AND RULE 15A-6

Prohibitions relating to unregistered broker-dealer (Section 15(a)(1)) - a broker-dealer must be registered as according to the Securities Exchange Act of 1934.

Exemption of certain foreign brokers or dealers (Rule 15a-6) - certain foreign broker-dealers are exempt from the registration requirements in certain instances if the broker-dealer:

1. makes transactions with persons that have not been solicited by the broker-dealer
2. furnishes research reports to U.S. institutional investors
3. induces purchase or sale by a U.S. institutional investor
4. makes transactions through a registered broker-dealer, certain banks, certain foreign persons present in the U.S., certain U.S. agencies outside the U.S., or certain U.S. citizens outside the U.S

SECTION 15(B)(4)

Sanctions against brokers or dealers (Section 15(b)(4)) - the SEC will place limitations on the activities, functions, and operations, suspend for up to 12 months, or revoke registration for any broker-dealer if it is in the public interest. These sanctions can apply if the broker-dealer:

1. has made a false or misleading statement during application for registration
2. has been convicted within the ten years prior to registration of certain felonies or misdemeanors
3. is prevented by judgment or decree from a court to act as an investment advisor, underwriter, broker, dealer, or other securities professional
4. has willfully violated any provisions of, or has helped facilitate any other person to violate any provisions of, the Securities Act of 1933, the Investment Advisors Act of 1940, the Investment Company Act of 1940, the Commodity Exchange Act, or the Securities Exchange Act of 1934
5. is subject to an order from the SEC barring the person from being associated with a broker-dealer
6. has violated similar foreign sanctions
7. is subject to certain orders from State securities authorities

SECTION 15(B)(6)

Sanctions for person associated with broker or dealer (Section 15(b)(6)) - the SEC will place limitations on the activities, functions, and operations, suspend for up to 12 months, or bar such person from being associated with a broker-dealer if the person has:

1. has made a false or misleading statement during application for registration
2. has been convicted within the ten years prior to registration of certain felonies or misdemeanors
3. is prevented by judgment or decree from a court to act as an investment advisor, underwriter, broker, dealer, or other securities professional
4. has willfully violated any provisions of, or has helped facilitate any other person to violate any provisions of, the Securities Act of 1933, the Investment Advisors Act of 1940, the Investment Company Act of 1940, the Commodity Exchange Act, or the Securities Exchange Act of 1934

SEA RULES 15c1-2, 15c1-3, AND 15c1-9

Fraud and misrepresentation (Rule 15c1-2) - it is prohibited to make untrue statements of material fact, or to omit to state a material fact with knowledge or reasonable grounds to believe that the statement is such.

Misrepresentation by brokers and dealers as to registration (Rule 15c1-3) - it is prohibited for a broker or dealer to represent that his registration is approval of the SEC of the financial standing or conduct of the business.

Use of pro forma balance sheets (Rule 15c1-9) - it is prohibited to use financial statements that project the receipt and application of proceeds from the sale or exchange of securities unless the assumptions upon which the statement is made are included in the caption in type that is at least as large as the font in the body of the statement.

SEA RULE 15c1-10

Customer - does not include a broker, dealer, or municipal securities dealer.

Completion of the transaction - the time when the customer pays the broker or dealer any part of the purchase price; if the customer makes payment in advance, the time the broker or dealer delivers the security to the customer; if the customer sells the security through a broker or dealer, the time the broker or dealer either receives the security from the customer or transfers the security out of the account of the customer; or if the customer sells the security through a broker or dealer and delivers the security in advance, the time when the broker or dealer makes payment into the account of the customer.

FINRA RULE 3160

Networking arrangements between members and financial institutions (FINRA Rule 3160) - a member that is a part of a networking agreement under which it conducts broker-dealer services on or off the premises of a financial institution is subject to the Rule.

Setting - the member is to be clearly identified and have its services distinguished from the services of the financial institution, have its name displayed where it conducts business, and maintain its services physically separate from that of the financial institution if at all possible.

Networking agreements - are to be governed by a written agreement with the responsibilities of the parties and compensations clearly detailed. The member is to ensure the agreement allows the supervisory personnel of the member to enter the premises of the financial institution.

Customer disclosure and written acknowledgment - when a customer opens an account with the member, it is to be disclosed in writing that the broker-dealer services are provided separately from the financial institution.

Communications with the public - all confirmations and account statements are to state that the services are being provided by the member. Any retail communications that include the location of the financial institution or promote the services of the financial institution must include disclosures that state "not FDIC insured," no bank guarantee," and "may lose value."

Notifications of terminations - if a member terminates an associated person that is in the employ of the financial institution for cause, the member is to inform the financial institution promptly.

Financial institution - federal and state chartered banks, savings and loan associations, savings banks, credit unions, and the service corporations of such institutions required by law.

Networking arrangement - contract or agreement between a member and a financial institution that allows the member to offer broker-dealer services on or off the premises of a financial institution.

Broker-dealer services - investment banking or securities business.

FINRA RULE 2310

Affiliate — a person who controls or is in common control with a member.

Cash available for distribution — cash flow minus restoration or creation reserves.

Cash flow — funds from all operations.

Direct participation program — a program that allows the owners pass-through taxation regardless of the type of legal entity.

Dissenting limited partner — a limited partner who objects to a limited partnership rollup transaction. Objection is in writing.

Equity interest — any stock in a corporation or ownership interest in a partnership.

Fair market net worth — all assets valued at market worth minus total liabilities.

Limited partner — a limited liability partner in a direct participation program who does not participate in the management decisions.

Limited partnership — a direct participation program with one or more general partners and one or more limited partners.

Limited partnership rollup transaction — certain combinations or reorganizations of limited partnership.

Management fee — fee paid for management and administration of a direct participation program.

Organization and offering expenses — all expenses from registering and offering interests in a direct participation program.

Participant — the person who buys an interest in a direct participation program.

Person — natural person or legal entity.

Prospectus — a document utilized for the purpose of announcing a security to the public.

Registration statement — a document that begins a registration of a security.

Solicitation expenses — direct marketing expenses.

Sponsor — a person who provides management for a direct participation program.

Transaction costs — any costs from carrying out the rollup transaction.

Application - no member is allowed to participate in the public offering of a direct participation program unless the program is in accordance with the Rule.

Suitability - a direct participation program is to have suitability standards established. Suitability standards are to determine that participants are in a suitable financial position to take advantage of the investment opportunity and can withstand the risk involved.

Disclosure - various disclosures are required to be given to the participant. Participant has the right to adequate and accurate material facts.

Organization and offering expense - the organization and offering expenses are all to be fair and reasonable.

Participation in rollups - there are various rules regarding rollups including:

1. Compensation - received by each member has to be equal regardless of the vote of said member, cannot exceed 2% of the exchange value of new securities, and has to be paid regardless of whether the member rejects the rollup.

2. Solicitation expense - has to be all paid by the proposing sponsor.
3. Fair and reasonable - any rollup transaction has to be fair and reasonable.

FINRA RULE 2330

A member is not to recommend to a customer, a deferred variable annuity unless the member believes that the customer has been informed of the features of deferred variable annuities, the customer would benefit from such features, and the specific annuity is suitable for the customer. The same standard applies to the exchange of a deferred variable annuity, but the member must also take into account any surrender charge, product enhancements, and other deferred variable annuities the customer may have had in the last 36 months. Prior to recommending, a member must make a reasonable effort to get important information from the customer material to investment decisions, such as age, income, financial situation, investment objectives, risk tolerance, etc. After receiving all information necessary to complete an application for a deferred variable annuity, it must be sent to an office of supervisory jurisdiction.

Application - this rule applies to recommended purchases and exchanges of deferred variable annuities and recommended initial subaccount allocations. The Rule states that documents can be created, stored, and transmitted in electronic or paper form, and electronic signatures are acceptable as well as written form.

Principal review and approval - before submitting a customer's application to an insurance company for processing, a member must have the application package approved by a registered principal.

Supervisory procedures - a member must implement procedures for surveillance to determine if associated persons have rates of effecting deferred variable annuity exchanges that raise for review, whether such rates are consistent with FINRA or SEC rules. A member must also have policies and procedures designed to implement corrective measures addressing inappropriate exchanges.

Training - a member must develop and document training policies or programs designed to ensure that associated persons who effect and registered persons who review transactions of deferred variable annuities are compliant.

NASD RULE 2830
COVERED ACCOUNT, PRIME RATE, RIGHTS OF ACCUMULATION, AND ASSET-BASED SALES CHARGE

Covered account - an account of an investment company or managed by an investment advisor of such company, or any account from which brokerage commissions are received as a result of request or direction of the principal underwriter of such company.

Prime rate - the most preferential interest rate on corporate loans in large U.S. money center commercial banks.

Rights of accumulation - a scale of reducing sales charges for the continuing purchases of a security.

Asset-based sales charge - a sales charge that is deducted from the net assets of an investment company. It does not include a service fee.

FRONT-END SALES CHARGE, DEFERRED SALES CHARGE, SERVICE FEE, FUND OF FUNDS, AND INVESTMENT COMPANIES IN A SINGLE COMPLEX

Front-end sales charge - a sales charge included in the public offering price of the shares of an investment company.

Deferred sales charge - an amount chargeable to sales or promotional expense paid by the shareholder after purchase but before or upon redemption.

Service fee - payments by an investment company for personal service or maintenance of shareholder accounts.

Fund of funds - an investment company that acquired securities issued by other investment companies.

Investment companies in a single complex - two or more companies that advertise themselves as one company for investment and investor services.

APPLICATION AND PROVISIONS

Application - the Rule applies to members' activities in securities of companies registered under the Investment Company Act of 1940, other than variable contracts subject to Rule 2820.

Conditions for discounts to dealers - a member, who is an underwriter of the securities in an investment company, may not sell such securities at a price other than the public offering price.

Selling dividends - a member may not state or imply that a purchase of recommended securities shortly before an ex-dividend date is advantageous unless there are clear tax or other advantages. Long-term capital gains cannot be represented as part of the income yield from an investment.

Withhold orders - a member may not withhold from placing a customer's order in order to profit for himself.

Purchase for existing orders - a member may not purchase from an underwriter the securities of an open-end investment company unless it is for the purpose of covering purchase order previously received or for its own investment.

Purchases as principal - a member who is party to a sales agreement may not purchase a security issued by an open-end management investment company or unit investment trust at a price lower that the bid price next quoted by the issuer.

Repurchase from dealer - a member who is a principal underwriter of a security may not repurchase securities from a dealer unless the dealer is a party to a sales agreement with a principal underwriter unless such dealer is the record owner of the security.

PROVISIONS IN SUB-PARAGRAPHS (1) - (5)

A member is not to favor or disfavor shares of a particular investment company based on commissions received.

A member is not to sell shares of an investment company if the member knows the investment company has an agreement under which the company directs portfolio securities transactions to a broker or dealer in consideration for promotion or sale of the company's shares.

A member is not to require brokerage commissions as a condition to the sale or distribution of shares in an investment company.

A member is not to offer to another member brokerage commissions as a condition to the sale or distribution of shares in an investment company.

A member is not to circulate information about the amount or level of commission received from an investment company other than to management personnel required to have such information.

PROVISIONS IN SUB-PARAGRAPHS (6) - (7)

A member is not to, as an underwriter of investment company shares, suggest, encourage, or sponsor an incentive campaign or sales effort of another member with respect to the shares of an investment company based on brokerage commissions of the underwriter-member.

A member is not to, in regards to retail sales or distribution of investment company shares:

1. provide sales personnel an incentive or additional compensation for the sale of specific investment companies based on the amount of brokerage commission received
2. recommend investment companies to sales personnel based on the amount of brokerage commission received
3. grant sales personnel participation in brokerage commission received
4. use sales of shares in any investment company as a factor in negotiating the price of or commissions to be paid on a transaction of an investment company

PROVISION REGARDING SALES CHARGE

Sales charge - a member is not to offer or sell shares of other certain types of investment companies with sales charges that are deemed to be excessive.

1. Refund of sales charge - if an issuer buys-back securities from a broker-dealer via an underwriter, the broker-dealer is to refund any concession received from the underwriter, and the underwriter is to pay the issuer any underwriter's share of the sales charge as well as any refund from a broker-dealer.
2. Disclosure of deferred sales charges - if a purchase or sale of an investment company share involves a deferred sales charge on redemption, a written confirmation must include "On selling your shares, you may pay a sales charge. For the charge and other fees, see the prospectus."

FINRA RULE 2342 AND NASD RULE 2830

"Breakpoint" sales (FINRA Rule 2342) - a member is not to sell investment company shares at a price below the point that the sales charge is reduced on quantity transactions in order to gain the applicable higher sales charges.

Prompt payment for investment company shares (NASD Rule 2830) - a member engaging in retail transactions for investment company shares are to transmit payments from customers for the shares to the payees by the later of either the end of the 3rd business day after the order to purchase, or the end of one business day after receipt of the payment from the customer.

SEA SECTION 3

As per Section 3 of the Securities Exchange Act of 1934, *security* — any note; stock; treasury stock; security future; security-based swap; bond; debenture; certificate of interest or participation in any profit-sharing agreement or in any oil, gas, or mineral royalty or lease; any collateral-trust certificate; preorganization certificate or subscription; transferable share; investment contract; voting trust certificate; certificate of deposit for a security; any put, call, straddle, option, or privilege on any security; any put, call, straddle, option, or privilege entered into on a national securities exchange relating to foreign currency, or in general, any instrument commonly known as a "security"; or any certificate of interest of participation in, temporary or interim certificate for, receipt for, or warrant or right to subscribe to or purchase any of the previous. It does not include currency, note, draft, bill of exchange, or banker's acceptance.

SECTION 3(A)(10) OF THE SEA

Any bond, note, debenture, or other debt security issued by a governmental unit that is payable from property or money which is used under a lease, sale, or loan arrangement by or for industrial or commercial enterprise is considered to be a separate security according to Section 3(a)(10) of the SEA. A security as described above is not a separate security and therefore exempt, if it is payable from general revenues of the governmental unit or the security relates to a public project.

SECTION 3 RULE 3A11-1

As per Section 3 of the Securities Exchange Act of 1934, equity security (Rule 3a11-1) - any stock or similar security, certificate of interest or participation in any profit sharing agreement, preorganization certificate or subscription, transferable share, voting trust certificate or certificate of deposit for an equity security, limited partnership interest, interest in a joint venture, or certificate of interest in a business trust; any security future on any such security; or any security convertible, with or without consideration into such a security, or carrying any warrant or right to subscribe to or purchase such a security; or any such warrant or right; or any put, call, straddle, or other option or privilege of buying such a security from or selling such a security to another without being bound to do so.

SECURITIES ACT OF 1933 – REGULATION A

Regulation A provides a registration exemption, as long as the below requirements are met:

1. Issuer - the issuer must be organized in the United States or Canada, may not be otherwise required to register, may not be a development stage company with no specific business plan, and may issue fractional undivided interests is oil rights and gas rights.
2. Aggregate offering price - total sales price cannot exceed $5,000,000.
3. Integration with other offerings - issue may not be integrated with certain other offerings.
4. Offering conditions - Form 1-A has to be filed with the SEC. No sales can be made until the 1-A has been qualified, a Preliminary Offering Circular is given to buyer in advance, and a Final Offering Circular is given to buyer with confirmation of sale or earlier.

INVESTMENT COMPANY ACT OF 1940

SECTION 2 – GENERAL DEFINITIONS

Advisory board — different from the board of directors or trustees, the members do not serve the company in any other capacity. The board advises but has no power to decide what the company purchases or sells.

Assignment — transfer of a contract.

Convicted — pertains to any verdict, judgment, etc. that has not been reversed.

Exchange — organization that provides a marketplace for the buying and selling of securities.

Face-amount certificate — a certificate that is an obligation of the issuer to pay a stated amount at a specific date.

Periodic payment plan certificate — a certificate that provides to the holder periodic payment and represents an interest in certain securities.

Promoter — is a person who has within the last year initiated or directed the organization of a company.

Redeemable security — a security that can be turned in for receipt of approximately a proportionate share of the company's assets.

Sales load — difference between the sales price of a security and the amount the company will use to invest.

Short-term paper — any note with a maturity less than nine months from being issued.

SECTIONS 3 AND 4

Definition of investment company - any company that engages primarily in investing, reinvesting, or trading securities; in issuing face-amount certificates of the installment type; or in investing, reinvesting, owning, holding, or trading securities and owns securities comprising 40% or more of the issuer's total assets.

Three classifications of investment companies:

1. Face-amount certificate company - a company engaged in issuing face-amount certificates of the installment type.
2. Unit investment trust - a company organized under a trust indenture, does not have a board of directors, and only issues redeemable securities. Does not include voting trusts.
3. Management company - any investment company other than a face-amount certificate company or a unit investment trust.

SECTION 5

Open-end companies vs. closed-end companies - an open-end company is a management company that is the issuer of its own redeemable securities. A closed-end company is a management company that is not an open-end company.

Diversified companies vs. non-diversified companies - a diversified company is a management company with at least 75% of its total asset value in cash, government securities, and securities of other investment companies in which not one issuer comprises more than 5% of the total value of the total management company asset value. A non-diversified company does not meet these requirements.

SECTION 8 AND 8(B)

Investment companies must register with the SEC. Form N-1A is the form used by open-end management companies. The registration statement is to include:

1. Policies on classifications and sub-classifications, borrowing money, the issuance of senior securities, engaging in the business of underwriting securities issued by others, concentrating investments in a particular industry, the purchase and sale of real estate and commodities, making loans, and portfolio turn-over.
2. All investment policies.
3. Any other fundamental policies.
4. Names and addresses of any affiliated person and a statement of business experience of each officer/director for the last five years.
5. All Securities Act and Securities Exchange Act required information and documents.

SECTION 11

Offers of exchange - it is illegal for a registered open-end company to make an offer to a security holder to exchange their security for another based on anything other than the relative net asset values, unless it has been approved by the commission.

SECTION 12

It is prohibited for an investment company to

1. purchase any security on margin
2. participate on a joint or joint and several basis in any securities trading account
3. affect a short sale of any security

Rule 12b-1 - Prohibits any registered open-end management investment company from being the distributor of any securities of which they are also the issuer, except for through an underwriter and if any payments made in connection with the distribution are made pursuant to a written plan outlining all the agreements relating to the distribution.

SECTION 13

Changes in investment policy - unless authorized by a vote, no investment company can:

1. Change its sub-classification.
2. Borrow money, issue senior securities, underwrite securities of another person, purchase or sell real estate or related commodities, in a manner deviating from the policy in the registration statement.
3. Deviate from the policy on concentration in certain industries as stated in the registration statement.
4. Change its business as to cease being classified as an investment company.

SECTION 19

A registered investment company may only make dividend payments from

1. accumulated undistributed net income, not including profits or losses realized upon sale of securities or properties
2. current net income, determined from the current or previous fiscal year

Statement regarding source of payment - if the source of dividend payment comes from another source, it must be accompanied by a statement regarding the source. The statement shall be on separate paper and is to indicate what percentage of the payment comes from net income, accumulated undistributed net profits, or paid-in surplus or other source (Rule 19a-1).

Distribution of long-term capital gains - long-term capital gains cannot be distributed more than once every 12 months (Rule 19b-1).

SECTION 22(C) AND RULE 22C-1

Regulation of underwriters and dealers by Commission (Section 22(c)) - the SEC can make rules applicable to registered investment companies, principal underwriters of or dealers in, redeemable securities of a registered investment company.

Pricing of redeemable securities for distribution, redemption and re- purchase (Rule 22c-1) - no registered investment company, principal underwriter of or dealer in a security can sell, redeem, or repurchase the security, except at a price based on the current net asset value.

SECTION 22(D)

Persons to and through whom redeemable securities may be sold (Section 22(d)) - a registered investment company is to only sell redeemable securities through a principal underwriter or at a current public offering price described in the prospectus.

Exemption from Section 22(d) to permit sales of redeemable securities at prices which reflect sales loads set pursuant to a schedule (Rule 22d-1) - the sales price can vary from the public offering price stated in the prospectus, if it is to reflect the scheduled variation or elimination of the sales load.

Exemption from Section 22(d) for certain registered separate accounts (Rule 22d-2) - certain separate registered accounts are exempt in regards to variable annuity contracts issued by the account, if it is to reflect variations in the sales load or other administrative charge.

SECTION 22(E)

Suspension of rights of redemption (Section 22(e)) - a registered investment company is not to suspend the right of redemption or postpone the date of payment for more than seven days, unless the NYSE is unusually closed or trading is restricted; unless an emergency exists that it is not reasonable to dispose of or determine value of assets; or unless the SEC permits it for the protection of the security holders.

Exemption from Section 22(e) during annuity payment period of variable annuity contracts participation in certain registered separate accounts (Rule 22e-1) - a registered separate account is exempt from the provisions in Section 22(e) during the annuity payment period in respect to contracts under which payments are being made upon life contingencies.

SECTION 35

Unlawful representation - it is illegal for anyone to issue or sell a security of an investment company to imply that the security is guaranteed or recommended by the United States; has been insured by the FDIC; or that it is guaranteed by any bank.

Deceptive or misleading names - no investment company can use a company name or security name that the SEC finds deceptive or misleading.

SECTION 37

Larceny and embezzlement - a person guilty of larceny and embezzlement is guilty of a crime. Conviction or acquittal in a state bars prosecution in any other state.

TRUST INDENTURE ACT OF 1939

Purpose - the Trust Indenture Act of 1939 helps protects bond investors.

Basic provisions - a trustee must be appointed for all bond issues. In the case of insolvency, the trustee will make a claim on the issuer's assets on behalf of the bond investor. All bond issues over $5 million are required to have a written agreement between the issuer and the holder that includes various disclosures.

Necessity to safeguard - the national public interest and investor's interest in debt securities is adversely affected when

1. the obligor fails to provide a trustee.
2. the trustee does not have adequate rights and powers.
3. the trustee does not have adequate resources.

4. the obligor is not obligated to furnish adequate information as to its financial condition.
5. the indenture has provisions that are misleading and deceptive.
6. the investor cannot remedy any of the aforementioned items because they are not involved in the preparation of the issue.

Duties and responsibilities

1. Duties prior to default - trustee is only liable for duties as outlined in the indenture and can rely on the information therein.
2. Notice of default - trustee is to give all notice of defaults to the security holder.
3. Duties in Default - exercise the power given in the indenture.
4. Responsibilities - trustees can be found liable for being negligent in their responsibilities.

Reports by trustee - trustee is to disclose to security holder in intervals not more than 12 months the following information:

1. any change in eligibility and qualifications
2. any material relationship change
3. the character and amount of any advances made that are unpaid
4. any change to amount, interest rate, or maturity date of all indebtedness owed to it by obligor
5. any change to property and funds in its possession
6. any release of property subject to lien of indenture
7. any additional issue of indenture securities
8. any action taken by trustee under the indenture

FINRA RULE 4513

Record of written complaints (FINRA Rule 4513) - members are to maintain a file of all written customer complaints, record of the action taken by the member, and reference to the location of files containing correspondence related to the complaint for at least four years.

"Complaint" defined (FINRA Rule 4513) - any grievance by a customer, associated person, or person authorized to act on behalf of a customer in connection with any solicitation or execution of a transaction or disposition of securities of the customer.

FINRA RULE 4530

A member is required to report it within 30 calendar days if the member or an associated person:

1. has violated any governing laws, rules, regulations, or standards of conduct
2. is the subject of any written consumer complaint involving theft, misappropriation of funds or securities, or forgery
3. is named as a defendant in a proceeding alleging violation of the Exchange Act of other governing legislature
4. is denied registration or is expelled or otherwise disciplined by a regulatory body
5. is indicted, convicted, or pleads guilty to any felony, or misdemeanor involving the purchase or sale of securities, taking of false oath, theft, larceny, robbery, and other pertinent misdemeanors
6. is a director, controlling stockholder, or certain other officers of a broker, dealer, or investment company that was suspended, expelled, or had its registration denied or revoked
7. is a defendant in certain securities, commodities, or financial related litigations

8. is engaged in certain business transactions with a person that is statutorily disqualified as defined in the Exchange Act
9. is subject to certain disciplinary action

A member is to report information regarding written customer complaints by the fifteenth day of the month after it was received.

FINRA RULES 8310, 8311, AND 8312

Sanctions for violation of the rules (Rule 8310) - FINRA may impose sanctions on a member or person associated for violation of applicable laws, regulations, and rules of the government of regulatory organization. A sanction can be appealed via written application.

Effect of a suspension, revocation, cancellation, or bar (Rule 8311) - if FINRA imposes a suspension, revocation, cancellation, or bar upon a person associated with member, the member is not to allow such person to remain associated with him in any manner, including ceasing all pay, credit, salary, etc.

FINRA BrokerCheck Disclosure (Rule 8312) - upon request, FINRA is to release information regarding current or former members via BrokerCheck.

FINRA RULES 8320 AND 8330

Payment of fines, other monetary sanctions, or costs; summary action for failure to pay (Rule 8320) - any fines or monetary sanctions are to be paid to the Treasurer of FINRA. FINRA may suspend or expel a member that fails to pay a fine promptly or fails to terminate association with a person who fails to pay a fine. FINRA may revoke the registration of a person associated with a member if he fails to pay promptly a fine or monetary sanction after seven days notice in writing.

Cost of proceedings (Rule 8330) - a member or person associated who has been disciplined according Rule 8310 will bear the cost of the proceedings as deemed fair by the Adjudicator.

FINRA CODE OF PROCEDURE

Purpose and application- the Code of Procedure outlines the proceedings for disciplining a member or person associated; proceedings for regulating the activities of a member with financial or operational difficulties; proceedings for suspension, cancellation, bars, prohibitions, or limitations; and proceedings for obtaining relief from FINRA eligibility requirements.

FINRA RULE 9120

Definitions:

Adjudicator — a person or group that presides over a proceeding and renders a decision or recommendation.

Chief Hearing Officer — designated by the CEO of FINRA to manage the Office of Hearing Officers.

Counsel to the National Adjudicatory Council — an attorney of the Office of the General Counsel of FINRA responsible for advising the National Adjudicatory Council.

Extended Hearing Panel — an adjudicator that conducts an extended hearing.

Extended Proceeding Committee — an appellate adjudicator that participates in the National Adjudicatory Council's consideration of an extended proceeding.

General Counsel — the Chief Legal Officer of FINRA.

Head of Enforcement — the individual designated by the FINRA CEO to manage the Department of Enforcement.

Hearing Officer — an attorney employed by FINRA that acts in an adjudicative role regarding disciplinary proceedings.

Hearing Panel — an adjudicator that conducts a disciplinary proceeding.

Market Regulation Committee — a FINRA committee designated to consider federal securities laws and FINRA rules in relation to securities quotes, transaction execution and reporting, and trading practices.

Panelist — a member of an FINRA panel that is not a Hearing Officer.

Primary District Committee — the District Committee designated to provide a panelist for a disciplinary proceeding.

Statutory Disqualification Committee — a subcommittee of the National Adjudicatory Council that makes a recommended decision to grant or deny an application for relief from FINRA eligibility requirements.

FINRA RULE 9130

Service; filing of papers - a complaint is served on a party by the Department of Enforcement or the Department of Market Regulation. An order, notice, or decision is served on each party by an adjudicator. Any papers other than complaints, orders, notices, or decisions such as answers and motions are to be served by the party on whose behalf the papers were prepared. Papers can be serviced in person, by U.S. mail, or by courier. Papers that are to be filed with an adjudicator are deemed on time based on the time received or mailed, should be filed with the Office of Hearing Officers, and should include a certificate of service showing that the person was served. The format of papers filed is subject to specific requirements.

FINRA RULE 9140

In a proceeding, a person may appear on his own behalf or, subject to certain provisions, be represented by another person. If a representative of a person wishes to withdrawal from appearing as such a representative, he must file a motion to withdraw. Communications by a participant in a proceeding such as ex parte communications are prohibited, and any such communication would need to be disclosed. Formal rules of evidence do not apply in a proceeding. If the court desires to take notice of a matter, it is to permit any party to oppose or comment on the proposal to take notice. Subject to certain limitations, a party in a proceeding is allowed to make an oral or written motion. During a motion, the adjudicator has full authority to rule on a motion or other matter.

FINRA RULE 9210

Complaint and answer (Rule 9210) - the Office of Disciplinary Affairs gives authorization for FINRA to issue a complaint, and a disciplinary proceeding is deemed to have begun when a complaint is served and filed. A complaint is to be in writing and detail the alleged conduct. The Office of Hearing Officers records each complaint filed in FINRA's disciplinary proceeding docket. After a complaint has been filed, a Hearing Officer is designated to preside over the proceeding, and panelists are appointed. A respondent in a complaint is to give an answer within 25 days of being served with the complaint. FINRA may request that a respondent write a letter of acceptance, waiver, and consent, which would state that the member does not dispute the violation in the complaint, he waives the right to a hearing, and consents to the sanctions imposed. If a member writes such letter, it is accepted as final and completes the entire complaint, answer, and decision process. FINRA may reject such a letter.

FINRA RULES 9220 AND 9240

Request for hearing; extensions of time, postponements, adjournments (Rule 9220) - a respondent may request a hearing in his answer to a complaint. A Hearing Officer is to notify all parties of the date, time, and place of any hearing at least 28 days prior to the start of the hearing. A Hearing Officer has the authority to extend or shorten any time limits required in the Code, including postponing or adjourning a hearing.

Pre-hearing conference and submission (Rule 9240) - a Hearing Officer may order parties to meet in a pre-hearing conference for the purpose of expediting the proceeding, establishing procedures, or improving the quality of the hearing. The Hearing Officer may also order parties to provide certain information before a hearing.

FINRA RULES 9230 AND 9250

Appointment of hearing panel, extended hearing panel (Rule 9230) - the Chief Hearing Officer appoints the Hearing Panel. It is to be composed of a Hearing Officer, which will chair the panel, and two panelists. A person qualified to be a panelist may be appointed as an observer. An observer can be present at the proceedings, but does not vote or participate in any administration of the proceeding. The Chief Hearing Officer will select a replacement panelist when necessary. A panelist can remove himself by recusal, and panelists can be removed by a party's motion to disqualify said panelist.

Discovery (Rule 9250) - FINRA is to make available to a respondent any documents connected with the investigation, with some exceptions when a document will be withheld. The Hearing Officer can require a copy of the list of withheld documents, and can rule that any document on the list be released for inspection.

FINRA RULE 9260

Hearing and decision (Rule 9260) - no later than ten days before a hearing, parties are to submit copies of evidence and names of witnesses. A person giving testimony is to take an oath. A Hearing Officer may exclude evidence that is irrelevant, immaterial, unduly repetitious, or unduly prejudicial. A hearing is recorded by a court reporter. Within 60 days after the final date for filings, conclusions, and briefs, the Hearing Officer is to prepare a written decision. This decision is posted on the Central Registration Depository, and copies are sent to any member the respondent is associated with.

FINRA RULES 9270 AND 9280

Settlement procedure (Rule 9270) - a respondent may propose a settlement at any time, which can be accepted or denied. A proceeding is concluded when the order of acceptance is issued.

Contemptuous conduct (Rule 9280) - if a party acts contemptuously during a proceeding, the Hearing Officer or panel may impose certain sanctions or, if an attorney, bar the person from representing others.

FINRA RULES 9310 AND 9340

Appeal to or review by National Adjudicatory Council (Rule 9310) - a respondent or certain FINRA departments may file for an appeal within 25 days after a decision. Such a filing will stay that subject decision. Certain decisions may be called for a review by the National Adjudicatory Council within 45 days after the service of decision.

Proceedings (Rule 9340) - a party may request an oral argument in front of a committee. All parties are required to attend the oral argument. Each party's oral argument is to be limited to 30 minutes. The oral arguments are recorded by a court reporter. The review is limited to the consideration of matters of record and oral arguments. The national Adjudicatory Council, after considering all matters in the review, will affirm, dismiss, modify, or reverse the decision of the hearing panel during the disciplinary proceeding.

FINRA RULES 9350, 9360, AND 9370

Discretionary review by FINRA Board (Rule 9350) - a governor may call for review of a proceeding by the FINRA Board. The FINRA Board may affirm, modify, reverse, increase, or reduce any sanction, or impose any other fitting sanction.

Effectiveness of sanctions (Rule 9360) - a sanction is effective as of a date determined by FINRA. A bar, expulsion, or permanent cease and desist order is effective upon the servicing of the decision.

Application to SEC for review (Rule 9370) - a respondent may apply for a review of a FINRA decision by the SEC. The filing of such application stays the effectiveness of the sanction.

FINRA RULES 9840 AND 9870

Issuance of temporary cease-and-desist order by hearing panel (Rule 9840) - the panel is to issue a decision not later than ten days after hearing the transcript. A temporary cease-and-desist order may be imposed if there is a preponderance of evidence for the alleged allegation and the conduct is likely to result in significant dissipation or conversion of assets or other significant harm to investors prior to the end of the disciplinary proceedings.

Application to SEC for review (Rule 9870) - a temporary cease-and-desist order can be reviewed by the SEC if the respondent files for such. Such a filing does not stay the effectiveness of the order.

FINRA IM-12000 AND IM-13000

Failure to act under provisions of Code of Arbitration procedure for customer/industry disputes (IM-12000 and IM-13000) - it may be deemed inconsistent with just and equitable principles of trade, and a violation of FINRA rules, to fail to comply with the Code of Arbitration Procedure for Customer/Industry Disputes.

RULES 12105 AND 13105

Agreement of the parties (Rules 12105 and 13105) - if the Code allows it, the parties may agree to modify a provision of the Code, but the written agreement of all named parties is required.

RULES 12200, 12201, 12202, 12204, AND 13204

Arbitration under an arbitration agreement or the rules of FINRA (Rule 12200) - a dispute between parties must be arbitrated if it is required by written agreement or requested by the customer; if the dispute is between a customer and a member; and if the dispute is in connection with business activities of the member.

Elective arbitration (Rule 12201) - parties may elect to arbitrate a dispute if the parties agree in writing; if the dispute is between a customer and a member; and if the dispute is in connection with business activities of the member.

Claims against inactive members (Rule 12202) - a claim against an inactive member is ineligible for arbitration unless the customer agrees in writing.

Class action claims (Rules 12204 and 13204) - class action claims cannot be arbitrated under the Code.

RULES 12205, 13200, 13201, AND 13202

Shareholder derivative actions (Rule 12205) - shareholder derivative actions may not be arbitrated under the Code.

Required arbitration (Rule 13200) - in regards to industry disputes, a dispute must be arbitrated if it is in connections with the business activities of a member and is between members, members and associated persons, or associated persons.

Statutory employment discrimination claims (Rule 13201) - these types of claims are not required to be arbitrated, but may be if the parties agree.

Claims involving registered clearing agencies (Rule 13202) - if a registered clearing agency has an agreement with FINRA to use its arbitration facilities and procedures, any dispute involving the agency is to be arbitrated according with the agreement and the rule of the clearing agency.

RULES 12800, 13800, 12801, AND 13801

Simplified arbitration (Rules 12800 and 13800) - if an arbitration involves less than $50,000, it can be arbitrated as a simplified arbitration. Simplified arbitrations involve a single arbitrator and no hearing unless requested. The parties can request documents from each other.

Default proceedings (Rules 12801 and 13801) - a claimant can request a default proceeding against certain respondents who fail to file an answer as per the Code. No hearings are held.

FINRA RULES 14104, 14105, AND 14109

Mediation under the Code (Rule 14104) - mediation is voluntary, and requires written agreement from all parties. Any matter that is eligible for arbitration may be mediated, if all parties agree.

Effect of mediation on arbitration proceedings (Rule 14105) - unless the parties agree, a mediation will not delay an arbitration pending FINRA.

Mediation ground rules (Rule 14109) - mediation is voluntary, and a party may withdrawal. The mediator is to be a neutral 3rd party and does not have authority to make decisions. All parties are to initially meet with the mediator to determine to course of the proceedings. The parties agree in good faith to come to a settlement. Mediation is private and confidential.

NASD RULE 1090

Foreign members (NASD Rule 1090) - if a member does not have an office in the United States that prepares and maintains financial and other reports required by the Commission and the Association, he must:

1. prepare such reports and maintain a general ledger and a description thereof in English and in U.S. dollars
2. reimburse the Association for any additional expenses from examining the member relating to the additional distance
3. ensure the availability of an English speaking person knowledgeable in securities and financial matters
4. utilize a broker/dealer registered with the Commission, a bank or clearing agency registered with the Commission located in the U.S., for all clearing transactions

SECTION 11 OF THE SECURITIES EXCHANGE ACT OF 1934

Regulation of floor trading - no member of a national securities exchange can transact in any security while on the floor of the exchange on his own account, or in an account in which the member has trading discretion, with some exception (Rule 11a-1).

Transactions yielding priority, parity and precedence - a transaction in the account of a member of a national securities exchange shall give priority to a transaction of a non-member in the order of processing (Rule 11a1-1(T)).

Transactions for certain accounts of associated persons of members - a transaction by a member for the account of an associated person is deemed to be prohibited as found in Rule 11a-1 (Rule 11a1-2).

Bona fide hedge transactions in certain securities - a bona fide hedge transaction by a member for its own account or the account of an associated person is deemed to be consistent with Rule 11a-1 and is a prohibited transaction (Rule 11a1-3(T)).

Bond transactions on national securities exchanges - a bond transaction on a national securities exchange by a member for his own account, or the account of an associated person, is deemed to be consistent with Rule 11a-1 and is a prohibited transaction (Rule 11a1-4(T)).

Transactions by registered competitive market makers and registered equity market makers - transactions by a NYSE-registered competitive market maker or an ASE-registered equity market maker are deemed to be subject to Rule 11a-1 (Rule 11a1-5).

Transactions effected by exchange members through other members - a member may transact in a security for his own account in specific situations when the order is executed by another member who is not an associated person (Rule 11a2-2(T)).

RULE 15c2-1 AND AGGREGATE INDEBTEDNESS

General provisions - a broker or dealer is prohibited from hypothecating any securities carried in the account of a customer if the circumstances permit:

1. the commingling of the customer's securities with other customer's securities, without the written consent of the customers;
2. the securities to be commingled with the account of another person that is not a bona fide customer of the broker or dealer; or
3. the securities to be hypothecated for an amount that exceeds the total indebtedness of all customers in respect of securities carried for their accounts.

Aggregate indebtedness - is not to be reduced because of uncollected items. To calculate, related guaranteed and guarantor accounts are treated as a single account, and balances carrying both long and short positions are adjusted by treating the market value of the securities required to cover any short position as though the market value were a debit.

SEC RULE 15c3-1

MINIMUM NET CAPITAL REQUIREMENTS

Every broker or dealer is to have a minimum net capital amount that does not allow the aggregate indebtedness to exceed 1500% of its net capital, or another minimum net capital requirement amount as specified below, whichever is greater.

1. Broker-dealers who carry customer accounts - at least $250,000.
2. Broker-dealers who carry accounts but do not hold customer funds or securities and operate under Paragraph (k)(2)(i) exemption of Rule 15c3-3 - at least $100,000.
3. Market makers - at least $2,500 for each security for which it is a market maker.
4. Dealers - at least $100,000.

Introducing broker-dealers

1. Firms that introduce accounts on a fully disclosed basis to another broker or dealer and do not receive funds or securities - at least $5,000.
2. Firms that introduce accounts on a fully disclosed basis to another broker or dealer and receive—but do not hold—customer or other broker-dealer securities and do not receive funds - at least $50,000.

Mutual fund brokers or dealers transacting a business in redeemable shares of registered investment companies and certain other share accounts - at least $25,000. A broker or dealer under this net capital requirement must promptly transmit all funds and deliver securities (on a wire order basis) and may not otherwise hold funds or securities for customers (subscription basis).

DEBT-EQUITY REQUIREMENT AND WITHDRAWAL OF EQUITY CAPITAL PROVISION

Debt-equity requirement - no broker or dealer is to allow his outstanding principal amount of satisfactory subordination agreements to exceed 70% of his debt-equity total for longer than 90 days.

Withdrawal of equity capital - a broker's or dealer's equity capital cannot be withdrawn by a stockholder or partner, nor by redemption or repurchase of stock, nor through payment of dividends; nor may there be any unsecured advance or loan made without written notice.

SATISFACTORY SUBORDINATION AGREEMENT AND COLLATERAL VALUE

A satisfactory subordination agreement is a subordination agreement that meets certain minimum requirements as outlined in SEC Rule 15c3-1d. A subordination agreement can be either a subordinated loan agreement or a secured demand note agreement.

1. Subordinated loan agreement - governs a subordinated borrowing of cash.
2. Secured demand note agreement - governs the contribution of a secured demand note to a broker or dealer and the pledge of securities or cash used to collateralize payment.

Collateral value - in regards to a security pledged to secure a secured demand note, collateral value is the market value of the security after a percentage deduction.

MINIMUM REQUIREMENTS OF SUBORDINATION AGREEMENTS

Minimum requirements of subordination agreements - According to SEC Rule 15c3-1d, a subordination agreement is to be for a minimum of one year and it is a valid and binding obligation. It is to be for a specified amount, and it is to effectively subordinate the right of the lender to receive any payment, to the claims of other creditors. The agreement is to provide that the cash proceeds of the agreement will be part of the broker's dealer's capital and are subject to business risk. The agreement is to give the broker or dealer the right to deposit any cash proceeds of the agreement to secure a demand note; pledge and hypothecate the securities pledged as capital; and lend to himself or others, the securities and cash pledged as collateral to secure a demand note.

TEMPORARY AND REVOLVING SUBORDINATION AGREEMENTS AND FILING REQUIREMENTS

Temporary and revolving subordination agreements - According to SEC Rule 15c3-1d, a broker or dealer is allowed, though not more than three times in a 12-month period, to enter into a temporary subordination agreement of no longer than 45 days, in order to enable the broker or dealer to participate as an underwriter or securities or other activities. A broker or dealer is allowed to enter into a revolving subordinated loan agreement that provides for prepayment within less than one year at the option of the broker or dealer upon written approval of the examining authority.

Filing requirements - two copies of any proposed subordination agreement are to be filed with the SEC at least ten days before the proposed execution date.

AGGREGATE INDEBTEDNESS, NET CAPITAL, AND HAIRCUTS

Aggregate indebtedness - the total unsecured and other customer related debt that a firm has. Aggregate indebtedness is used in determining minimum net capital requirements.

Net capital - net capital is general considered to be a firm's total assets minus total liabilities. Adjustments are typically made for illiquid assets - assets that are not easily convertible into cash. Securities are usually treated differently from other assets when computing net capital. Securities are given "haircuts."

Haircuts - securities are given haircuts when computing net capital. Their value is reduced from the current market value because of the volatile nature of securities' market values. Some securities carry additional haircuts because of a limited market, unduly concentrated positions, or because of being non-marketable.

ALTERNATIVE NET CAPITAL REQUIREMENT

A broker or dealer may elect to not be subject to the aggregate indebtedness standard of computing its minimum net capital requirement in lieu of using the alternative standard. Under the alternative standard, a broker or dealer is not to allow its net capital to be less than the greater of either

$250,000 or 2% of aggregate debit items. The broker's or dealer's examining authority must be notified.

SEC RULE 15c3-2

A broker or dealer is not to use the funds from any customer's free credit balance in connection with the operation of the broker's or dealer's business, unless there have been established adequate procedures under which a customer is sent, every three months, a written statement informing him of the amount due to the customer on the statement date. The broker or dealer shall also notify the customer that the funds are not segregated and may be used in business operations and that the funds are payable on demand to the customer.

SEC RULE 15c3-3

Definitions

1. Excess margin securities - margin securities in a customer account that have a market value of more than 140% of the total debit balances in a customer's margin account that are not margin securities.
2. Qualified security - a security issued or guaranteed by the United States.
3. Free credit balance - a broker or dealer liability which is payable to a customer on demand.

Physical possession or control of securities - a broker or dealer is to physically obtain and maintain control of all fully paid for securities and excess margin securities carried for a customer.

REQUIREMENT TO REDUCE SECURITIES TO POSSESSION OR CONTROL

No later than the next business day, a broker or dealer is to determine the quantity of fully paid securities and excess margin securities in its possession or control and those not in its possession or control. If a broker or dealer determines that there are fully paid-for securities or excess margin securities of which he is not in possession and control, he must make certain efforts to remedy the situation.

SPECIAL RESERVE BANK ACCOUNT FOR THE EXCLUSIVE BENEFIT OF CUSTOMERS

When deposits are required, a broker or dealer is to have a special reserve bank account for the exclusive benefit of customers. This account is to be separate from any other account and is to contain a reserve amount of cash and/or securities as stipulated in Rule 15c3-3a.

NOTIFICATION OF BANKS

A broker or dealer with a special reserve bank account is to receive a notice from the bank that the bank has been notified that all cash and securities deposited therein are for the exclusive benefit of customers and are being kept separate from any of the broker's or dealer's other bank accounts. The notice shall also state that the funds will not be used as security for a loan to the broker or dealer and is not subject to any right, charge, security interest, lien, or claim of any kind of favor of the bank.

WITHDRAWALS FROM THE RESERVE BANK ACCOUNT, BUY-IN OF SHORT SECURITY DIFFERENCES, AND EXEMPTIONS TO THE RULE

Withdrawals from the reserve bank account - a broker or dealer can make a withdrawal from the special reserve bank account only if the remaining amount is not less than the required minimum.

Buy-in of short security differences - a broker or dealer is to buy-in all short security differences found during examination, count, verification, and comparison within 45 days.

Exemptions under subsection (k) - the Rule does not apply to certain brokers and dealers if they meet certain transaction criteria, such as trading only in securities of certain investment companies.

DELIVERY OF FULLY PAID AND EXCESS MARGIN SECURITIES, COMPLETION OF SELL ORDERS ON BEHALF OF CUSTOMERS, AND EXTENSIONS OF TIME

Delivery of fully paid and excess margin securities - a customer has the right to demand the physical delivery of a security certificate for fully paid-for securities and margin securities upon customer's full payment.

Completion of sell orders on behalf of customers - if ten days after executing a sell order for a customer a broker or dealer has not received the subject securities from the customer, the broker or dealer is to close the transaction with the customer by making a mandatory buy-in.

Extensions of time - time periods stated in the Rule may be extended by the SEC if it is believed the broker or dealer is acting in good faith and exceptional circumstances warrant it.

LOSS OF 15C3-3(K) EXEMPTION

Approval of Change in Exempt Status under SEC Rule 15c3-3 (NASD Rule 3140) - a member can lose its 15c3-3(k) exemption when the member conducts business that will change its exempted status without the prior written approval of the NASD.

FINRA RULE 4521

Notifications, questionnaires and reports (FINRA Rule 4521) - every carrying or clearing member of FINRA must submit financial and operational information as FINRA deems essential. Every member subject to the alternative method of computing net capital is to file such supplemental reports prescribed by FINRA. Every carrying or clearing member is to notify FINRA within 48 hours after his tentative net capital has declined 20% or more. Members carrying margin accounts are to submit a report containing the total of all debit balances in securities margin accounts and the total of all free credit balances in all cash and securities margin accounts, on a settlement date basis.

SEC SECTION 17
RULE 17A-3

According to SEC Rule 17a-3 regarding records to be made by certain exchange members, brokers and dealers, brokers and dealers are required to maintain the following books and/or records:

- Memorandum of each brokerage order given or received for the purchase or sale of securities (for customer and firm accounts) - whether executed or unexecuted. The memorandum is to show the terms and conditions; the account for which entered; the time the order was received; the time of entry; the price it was executed; the identity of any associated persons responsible for the account; the identity of the person who entered or accepted the order; and the time of execution or cancellation.
- Memorandum of each purchase and sale for the account of the firm - including the price, the time of execution, and if the transaction was with a customer other than a broker or dealer, a memorandum of each order received showing the time of receipt, the terms and conditions; the identity of each associated person responsible for the account; and the identity of the person who entered or accepted the order.
- Blotters or other records of original entry - are to contain an itemized daily record of all purchases and sales of securities, all receipts and deliveries of securities, all receipts and disbursements of cash, as well as all other debits and credits.

- Copies of customer confirmations - and copies of notices of all other debits and credits for accounts of customers.
- Identification data on beneficial owners of all accounts - all cash and margin accounts are to have identification data including the name and address of the beneficial owner of the account.
- Ledgers or other records reflecting all assets and liabilities - including income and expense and capital accounts.

RULE 17A-4

Records to be preserved by certain exchange members, brokers and dealers (Rule 17a-4) - every broker and dealer is to keep general records for six years. For the first two years of record retention, the records are to be kept in an easily accessible place. Records of associated persons are to be kept until three years after the person's employment has terminated. Records can be produced or reproduced on micrographic media. If records are to be maintained by an outside service bureau, such bureau is to file with the Commission.

RULE 17A-5
MONTHLY AND QUARTERLY REPORTS

Every broker or dealer that clears or carries customer accounts is to file:

1. part 1 of Form X-17A-5 within ten business after the end of each month.
2. part 2 of Form X-17A-5 within 17 business days after the end of each quarter and within 17 business days after the annual audit of financial statements.

Every broker or dealer who does not clear or carry customer accounts is to file Part 2A of Form X-17A-5 within 17 business days after the end of each quarter and within 17 business days after the annual audit of financial statements.

Certain brokers or dealers who calculate their capital charges according to Rule 15c3-1e must file additional reports.

REPORT FILED UPON TERMINATION OF MEMBERSHIP INTEREST

If a broker or dealer with a membership in a national securities exchange or registered national securities association is no longer in good standing, the broker or dealer is—within two days of the event—to file Part 2 and Part 2A of Form X-17A-5 with the SEC.

CUSTOMER STATEMENTS

Every broker or dealer is to send to his customers, and file with the SEC, the following unaudited statements within 65 days of the date of the statement: balance sheet, a net capital statement footnote, and a statement of availability of the Statement of Financial Condition. For purposes of this rule, the term "customer" means any person who is not a broker, dealer, partner or officer of a broker or dealer, or certain persons with claim to the capital of a broker or dealer.

ANNUAL FILING OF AUDITED FINANCIAL STATEMENTS

Annually a broker or dealer is to file a report that has been audited by an independent public accountant. This report is to contain a Statement of Financial Condition, a Statement of Income, a Statement of Cash Flows, a Statement of Changes in Stockholders' Equity, and a Statement of Changes in Liabilities Subordinated to Claims of General Creditors.

QUALIFICATION OF ACCOUNTANTS AND AUDIT OBJECTIVES

- *Qualification of accountants* - in order to be recognized by the Commission, an accountant must be registered, in good standing, and entitled to practice.
- *Audit objectives* - the audit should following generally accepted auditing standards, and is to include audits of the accounting system, the internal accounting control, and procedures for safeguarding securities.

TECHNICAL REQUIREMENTS, REPRESENTATIONS AS TO THE AUDIT, AND OPINION TO BE EXPRESSED

- *Technical requirements* - the accountant's report is to be dated and manually signed. It is to indicate the city and state and detail the financial statements and schedules covered by the report.
- *Representations as to the audit* - the report shall state whether the audit followed generally accepted auditing standards; state whether the accountant reviewed the procedures for safeguarding securities; and designate auditing procedures deemed necessary that have been omitted and why.
- *Opinion to be expressed* - the report is to clearly state the opinion of the accountant in regards to financial statements and schedules and in regards to the consistency of the application of the accounting principles.

ACCOUNTANT'S REPORT ON MATERIAL INADEQUACIES, EXTENSIONS AND EXEMPTIONS, NOTIFICATION OF CHANGES OF FISCAL YEAR, AND FILING REQUIREMENTS

- *Accountant's report on material inadequacies* - a supplemental report is to accompany the filing of the annual audit report that describes any material inadequacies found to exist during the audit.
- *Extensions and exemptions* - a broker's or dealer's annual filing dates may be extended by an examining authority. Exemptions may be given to certain banks and insurance companies. The SEC has the authority to grant any extension or exemption. A broker or dealer is exempt from the Rule if he is not a member of a national securities exchange or registered national securities association.
- *Notification of changes of fiscal year* - if a broker or dealer decides it is necessary to change his fiscal year, a notice of such must be filed with the SEC.
- *Filing requirements* - filings are deemed to have been accomplished when they are received by the SEC.

RULE 17A-11

Notification provisions for brokers and dealers - a broker or dealer is to give notice the day of, if his net capital declines below the required minimum amount stated in Rule 15c3-1. A broker or dealer is to give notice within 24 hours if his aggregate indebtedness or net capital pass certain threshold levels detailed in the Rule. A broker or dealer is to give notice on the same day if he fails to keep current the required books and records. A broker or dealer is to give notice within 24 hours of the discovery of a material inadequacy and transmit a report within 48 hours stating what is being done to correct the situation.

RULE 17A-13

Quarterly security counts to be made by certain exchange members, brokers and dealers (Rule 17a-13) - a broker or dealer, unless exempt from the Rule based on the nature of his transactions, is—in each calendar quarter year—to:

1. physically examine and count all securities held
2. account for all securities in his control or direction but not in his physical possession
3. verify all securities in his control or direction but not in his physical possession that have been in such status for longer than 30 days
4. compare results of count and verification with records
5. record on the books and records all unresolved differences

Persons to perform or supervise required securities counts - the examination, count, verification, and comparison are to be made or supervised by persons who in their regular duties do not have direct responsibility for the care and protection of the securities or the making or preservation of the subject records.

RULE 17F-1
REPORTING INSTITUTION

The definition of reporting institution includes every national securities exchange and its members, registered securities association, broker, dealer, municipal securities dealer, government securities broker, government securities dealer, registered transfer agent, registered clearing agency and participants, member of the Federal Reserve System, and bank with deposits insured by the FDIC.

REPORTING REQUIREMENTS

All reporting agencies are to report to the SEC the following within 1 business day:

1. the theft or loss of any securities certificates believed to be based in criminal activity
2. any missing or lost securities certificates that have been misplaced for a period of two days and not believed to be based in criminal activity
3. any counterfeit securities discovered. This is also to be reported to the FBI

REQUIRED AND PERMISSIVE INQUIRIES

Required inquiries - every reporting institution is to inquire of the SEC for every security received to determine if it has been reported as missing, lost, counterfeit, or stolen, with some exception.

Permissive inquiries - even when a report or inquiry is not required by this Rule, any reporting institution may report to or inquire of the SEC regarding any security certificate.

FINRA RULE 4511

Members are to maintain all books and records according to FINRA and SEC rules and keep them for at least six years in a format that complies with Rule 17a-4 of the Securities Exchange Act of 1934.

FINRA RULE 2261

Disclosure of financial condition (FINRA Rule 2261) - a member is required to furnish recent financial statements to other members upon request when the member is party to an open transaction or has on deposit cash or securities of another member.

FINRA RULES 4110 AND 4120

Capital compliance (FINRA Rule 4110) - for the safety of public interest, FINRA may at any time impose a capital requirement that is greater than what would ordinarily be required. If a member is not compliant with capital requirements he must suspend all business operations.

Regulatory notification and business curtailment (FINRA Rule 4120) - a FINRA member is to notify FINRA within 24 hours if his capital requirement falls below certain thresholds. If a member does not meet the capital thresholds for a period of 15 days or more, it is not permitted to expand its business during this time period. A member is required to reduce his business until he meets the capital requirements.

FINRA RULE 4230

FINRA is the examining authority for a member clearing firm, the member must submit requests for extension of the time limit for margin calls to be satisfied.

FINRA RULE 4311

A member must not agree to the carrying of a customer account unless the agreement is with another FINRA member. A member is to submit to FINRA for prior approval before entering into an agreement for carrying of accounts. The agreement must allocate the specific responsibilities of opening and approving accounts; acceptance of orders; transmission of orders for execution; execution of orders; extension of credit; receipt and delivery of funds and securities; preparation and transmission of confirmations; maintenance of books and records; and monitoring of accounts. The carrying firm must take the responsibility of safeguarding funds. A customer is to receive upon the opening of an account, a written notice of any carrying agreement.

FINRA RULE 4360

Coverage required - a member with a net capital requirement of less than $250,000 must maintain at least the greater of 120% of the net capital requirement or $100,000 in fidelity bond coverage.

Deductible provision - there may be in a fidelity bond a provision providing a deductible of up to 25% of the coverage purchased. If it is greater than 10%, this amount must be deducted from the member's net worth.

Annual review of coverage - a member is to annually review the adequacy of the coverage and make any necessary adjustments.

Notification of change - a member is to notify FINRA immediately if his fidelity bond is cancelled, terminated, or substantially modified.

Substantially modified - a change in the type or amount of a bond that makes it no longer complaint with the Rule.

FINRA RULE 5330 AND FINRA RULE 4560

Adjustment of orders (FINRA Rule 5330) - When a member holds an order from another broker-dealer, the member is to adjust the price and/or number of shares to compensate for any dividend, payment, or distribution on the day of the quote for the security, according to guidelines outlined in the Rule.

Short-interest reporting (FINRA Rule 4560) - members are to maintain records of all of the short equity positions in all accounts and report regularly to FINRA such information.

FINRA RULE 4521 AND NASD RULE 3150

Notifications, questionnaires and reports (FINRA Rule 4521):

1. Every member is to submit to FINRA in the form and time specified by FINRA, financial and operational information regarding the member for the protection of investors and the public.
2. Members approved to use the alternative method of computing net capital (as per SEA Rule 15c3-1) is to file supplemental and alternative reports as prescribed by FINRA.
3. Each carrying or clearing member is to notify FINRA in writing within 48 hours after his tentative net capital has declined 20% or more.
4. Each member who maintains margin accounts for customers must submit to FINRA monthly, a report containing the total of all debit balances in margin accounts, and the total of all free credit balances in cash accounts and margin accounts.

Reporting requirements for clearing firms (NASD Rule 3150):

Member clearing firms are to report to NASD, data pertaining to the member or the member for which it clears. The data should be easily discernible as to which data belongs to accounts of the introducing member or to accounts where the introducing member is a clearing intermediary.

SEC RULE 3A12-9

Certain direct participation programs where the purchase price is paid to the issuer in deferred payments are exempt from the restrictions regarding the extension of credit found in the Securities Exchange Act of 1934 in Section 7(c) and 11(d)(1), as long as certain provisions are met. These provisions include:

1. the deferred payments are reasonable considering the capital needs and program objectives
2. not less than 50% of the purchase price of the security is paid at the time of purchase
3. the total purchase price of the security is due within two or three years, depending on the program

SEC RULE 10B-16

Brokers and dealers who extend credit to customers must have processes to ensure that each customer:

A. Is given at or before the opening of an account, a written disclosure of the conditions under which an interest charge will be imposed; the annual rate of interest that can be imposed; the method of computing interest; whether or not rates are subject to change without prior notice; the method of determining credit balances; any other charges; and the nature of any interest or lien retained by the broker or dealer in the security of other property held as collateral.

B. Is given quarterly, a written statement of the balance at the beginning of the period including dates, amounts, and descriptions of all credits and debits; the total interest charge for the period; and any other charges.

SECTION 11(D)(1)

Section 11(d)(1) - Extension of credit - it is prohibited for a broker-dealer to extend or maintain credit for the purchase of a security that is part of a new issue in which the broker-dealer creditor participated as part of the selling syndicate.

Exemption from Section 11(d)(1) for certain investment company securities held by broker-dealers as collateral in margin accounts (Rule 11d1-2) - securities issued by certain registered open-end investment companies or unit investment trusts are exempt from the provisions of Section 11(d)(1) if the customer receiving credit has owned said security for more than 30 days, or the security is being purchased under an automatic reinvestment of dividends plan.

Exemption of certain securities from Section 11(d)(1) (Rule 11d-1) - a security is exempt from the provisions of 11(d)(1) if:

1. the broker-dealer has not sold or purchased the security to or from the customer's account
2. the security was acquired by the customer in an exchange with the issuer for an outstanding security of the same issuer on which credit was lawfully maintained for the customer
3. the customer is a broker, dealer, or bank
4. the security is acquired by the customer by exercising certain rights evidence by warrants or certificates
5. the broker-dealer has 50% or less of the specific class of securities and the security was sold or purchased to or from a customer's account on a day which the broker-dealer was not participating in the distribution of the security

SEC RULE 15c2-5

Disclosure and other requirements when extending or arranging credit in certain transactions (Rule 15c2-5) - if any broker or dealer is to sell a security to a customer for which he is extending credit for the transaction, the broker or dealer must deliver a written statement to the customer that outlines the customer's obligations under the loan arrangement; disclose the risks and disadvantages of the transaction; and disclose all commissions, discounts, or other remuneration received by the broker or dealer. The broker or dealer must also receive from the customer, information regarding his financial needs, and must determine if the arrangement is suitable for such a customer.

FINRA RULES 4140 AND 4521

Audit (FINRA Rule 4140) - FINRA may at any time direct a member to have an audit completed by an independent public accountant or according to other standards.

Notifications, questionnaires and reports (FINRA Rule 4521) - a carrying or clearing member is to submit to FINRA financial and operational information regarding the member that FINRA deems essential for the protection of investors and public interest. If a member is approved to use an alternative method of computing net capital, it must file supplemental and alternative reports. A carrying or clearing member is to notify FINRA within 48 hours if his tentative net capital has declined 20% or more.

REGULATION T

Regulation T discusses credit by brokers and dealers.

TERMS

The following are terms found in Regulation T:

- *Creditor* - broker/dealers that extend credit.
- *Customer* - a person to whom a creditor extends credit.
- *OTC margin stock* - any equity security traded over-the-counter that meets certain qualifications to be able to be treated as if it were traded on a national exchange.

- *Margin security* - any security traded on a national securities exchange; any security traded on the NASDAQ; any non-equity security; any security issued by certain investment companies; any foreign margin stock; and any debt security convertible into a margin security.
- *Exempted securities mutual fund* - a security issued by certain investment companies provided that the company has 95% of its assets in exempted securities.
- *Non-equity security* - a security that is not an equity security.

GENERAL PROVISIONS

Separation of accounts - requirements of an account may not be met by considering items in another account. If cash or securities are being withdrawn from one account to be used for another account to meet requirements, and it is permitted by Regulation T, written entries need to be made.

Maintenance of credit - credit once extended must be maintained, regardless of:

1. reductions in customer's equity from changing market prices
2. a security ceasing to be a margin or exempted security
3. a change in margin requirements

Guarantee of accounts - a customer's account cannot be guaranteed.

Receipt of funds or securities - a creditor can accept as immediate payment cash, checks, or securities. If a payment has been sent by another creditor, the funds can be considered received upon written notification from the creditor that it has been sent.

Arranging for loans by others - a creditor can arrange for credit to be extended to customers from another creditor.

MARGIN ACCOUNT

Margin transactions - a margin transaction is in essence buying securities on credit. For a broker/dealer, all customer transactions not otherwise specified are to be recorded in the margin account. Separate margin accounts for the same customer can be created in certain circumstances when different third party creditors or investment advisers are involved.

Liquidation in lieu of deposit - if a margin call is not met within the required time limit, the creditor is to liquidate a sufficient amount of the security to satisfy the outstanding margin requirement.

Withdrawals of cash or securities - cash and securities can be withdrawn from an account except if there is an outstanding requirement of cash or securities to be deposited, or if the withdrawal would create an additional margin requirement.

Short sale against the box - a short sale against the box is treated as a long sale when computing margin requirements.

When-issued securities - the required margin on a net long or net short commitment in a when-issued security is the same required margin as if the security were an issued margin security plus any unrealized loss and less any unrealized gain.

Stock used as cover - if a short position in a security serves in lieu of a required margin on a short put, the amount that needs to be added to the short sale margin is to be increased by any unrealized loss of the position.

Accounts of partners - partners of the creditor can have margin accounts, but the financial relationship with the firm must be disregarded when computing margin or equity.

Contribution to joint venture - if a margin account belongs to a joint venture in which the creditor is a part of, any interest that the creditor has in the account beyond its rights to share in the profits of the joint venture is to be considered an extension of credit.

Transfer of accounts - if an account is transferred from one creditor to another, the transferee can treat the account as if it were maintained by the transferee since inception, provided that the transferor provides a signed statement that any margin call has been satisfied.

Sound credit judgment - when determining the margin required, the creditor will make the decision for a specific security without giving regard to the customer's other assets or positions that are unrelated.

When additional margin is required - when computing deficiency, all transactions on the same day are combined to determine if any additional margin is required from the investor.

Satisfaction of deficiency - the additional required margin can be satisfied by a transfer from a special memorandum account or by cash, margin securities, or exempted securities.

Time limits - a margin call is to be satisfied within one payment period.

SPECIAL MEMORANDUM ACCOUNTS

A special memorandum account may be maintained in connection with a margin account and may contain dividend and interest payments; cash - including cash deposited to meet a margin call; certain proceeds from sales; and margin excess.

GOOD FAITH ACCOUNTS

Good faith account - a creditor may affect or finance customer transactions in a good faith account, as long as certain provisions are met. The transactions must be buying, carrying, or trading securities entitled to the good faith margin. Additional provisions include arbitrage, prime broker transactions, and non-purpose credit.

Arbitrage - in a good faith account a creditor can make bona fide arbitrage transactions. A bona fide arbitrage transaction is a:

1. purchase or sale of a security in one market simultaneously with an offsetting transaction in another market, in order to take advantage of the price difference in the markets.
2. a purchase of a security exchangeable or convertible within 90 days into a second security together with an offsetting sale of the second security at the same time, to take advantage of the price difference of the two securities.

Prime broker transactions - pursuant to SEC guidelines, a creditor can make transactions under a prime broker arrangement.

Non-purpose credit - credit that a creditor extends for effecting and carrying transactions in commodities and foreign exchanges. Creditors can extend and maintain non-purpose credit in certain instances.

BROKER-DEALER CREDIT ACCOUNT

Purchase or sale of security against full payment - a creditor can buy or sell securities from or to another creditor if he is under a good faith agreement to deliver promptly the full payment.

Joint back office - a creditor can affect or finance transactions for any of its owners as long as the creditor is a clearing and servicing broker or if the creditor is owned by any combination of other creditors.

Capital contribution - a creditor can extend credit to any of his owners or partners for the purpose of making a capital contribution to the creditor.

Emergency and subordinated credit - with approval of the appropriate authority, a creditor can extend credit to another creditor for emergency needs, and also can extend subordinated credit for capital purposes in certain instances.

Omnibus credit - a creditor can affect and finance transactions for a registered broker/dealer if such broker/dealer gives the creditor written notice that all securities are for customers and that any short sales transacted are on the behalf of customers only and not of partners of the broker/dealer.

Special purpose credit - a creditor can extend credit to:

1. finance the purchase or sale of securities for prompt delivery, if credit is repaid upon completion;
2. finance securities in transit, if credit is repaid upon completion;
3. enable a broker/dealer to purchase securities, if it is repaid on the same day;
4. an exempted borrower;
5. finance the activities of a registered market maker on a national securities exchange;
6. finance the activities of an underwriter registered on a national securities exchange.

CASH ACCOUNT

Permissible transactions: A creditor, in a customer cash account, may:

1. buy for, or sell to, any customer any security or asset as long as there are sufficient funds or if the creditor accepts the customer's agreement to pay promptly any necessary payments before selling the security or asset
2. buy from, or sell to, any customer any security or asset so long as the securities is actually held in the account or if the creditor accepts the customer's statement that the security is actually held by the customer and it will be deposited promptly
3. issue, endorse, guarantee, or sell an option for a customer as part of a covered option transaction
4. use escrow in lieu of cash in certain instances

Time periods for payment, cancellation, or liquidation - full cash payments are to be received from customer for purchases within 1 payment period of the transaction. A creditor is to cancel or liquidate any necessary portion of a transaction that the customer has not paid for.

90-day freeze - if a security is sold or transferred to another broker before being paid for in full, there will be a 90-day freeze during which the customer will not be able to make trades in the account before paying for them first.

Extension of time periods - in certain circumstances the time periods for payment, cancellation, or liquidation may be extended, or a waiver may be granted for the 90-day freeze.

BORROWING AND LENDING SECURITIES

A creditor can borrow or lend securities with the purpose of delivering the securities in case of short sales or similar situations. A creditor can trade foreign securities to a foreign person for any purpose that is lawful in that country. Exempted borrowers can freely lend securities.

REGULATION U AND REGULATION X

Purpose of Regulation U - Regulation U limits the amount of credit that a lender can extend for the purpose of use in margin accounts.

Purpose credit - purpose credit is any credit extended for purchasing or carrying margin stock.

Exceptions from general rule for broker-dealers - an exemption is offered in regards to special purpose loans to broker-dealers. A lender may extend credit to a broker-dealer, without regard to the rules set forth in Regulation U that would otherwise apply if the credit is for specific purposes such as hypothecation loans, temporary advances in payment-against-delivery transactions, loans for securities in transit or transfer, intra-day loans, arbitrage loans, market maker and specialist loans, underwriter loans, emergency loans, and capital contribution loans.

Regulation X restricts purpose credit limits borrowed from outside of the United States.

SARBANES-OXLEY ACT
CORPORATE RESPONSIBILITIES FOR FINANCIAL REPORTS

Corporate responsibility for financial reports - principal executive officers and the principal financial officer of a company filing reports under this title are to certify in each annual report that:

1. they have reviewed the report
2. the report does not contain any untruth about material facts
3. the financial information fairly presents the financial condition of the company
4. the signing officers are responsible for establishing and maintaining internal controls, have designed internal controls, have evaluated the effectiveness of the internal controls, and have presented in the report the conclusions about the effectiveness of the internal controls
5. the officers have indicated whether there were significant changes in the internal controls

Included in the internal controls could be the development, implementation and assessment of an ethics course.

DISCLOSURES IN PERIODIC REPORTS AND ENHANCED CONFLICT OF INTEREST PROVISIONS

Disclosures in periodic report - pro forma financial information contained in reports or public disclosures are to be presented in a manner that does not contain any untrue statements or material facts and that reconciles it with the financial condition under generally accepted accounting principles.

Enhanced conflict of interest provisions - an issuer may not extend credit to one of its officers in the form of a personal loan.

DISCLOSURES OF TRANSACTIONS INVOLVING MANAGEMENT AND PRINCIPAL STOCKHOLDERS

Disclosures of transactions involving management and principal stockholders - directors, officers, and principal stockholders who are beneficial owners of more than 10% of any class of equity security are to file a statement electronically with the SEC either at the time the security is registered, within ten days of becoming a 10% owner, or in the case of a change in ownership, before the end of the second business day after the transaction. The statement is to contain information regarding the amount of all equity securities owned and the ownership of the person filing.

MANAGEMENT ASSESSMENT OF INTERNAL CONTROLS

Management assessment of internal controls - management is responsible for establishing, maintaining, and assessing the effectiveness of internal controls and procedures for financial reporting. Any registered public accounting firm that prepares or issues audit reports for the issuer is to attest to the assessment made by the management of the issuer.

INSIDER TRADING AND SECURITIES FRAUD ENFORCEMENT ACT OF 1988
SECTION 3

Civil penalties of controlling persons for illegal insider trading by controlled persons - Section 3 of the Insider Trading and Securities Fraud Enforcement Act of 1988 makes small amendments to Section 21(d) of the Securities Exchange Act of 1934. It also adds Section 21A to the same, and Section 204A to the Investment Advisers Act of 1940.

Investment Advisers Act of 1940

1. Section 204 — Annual and other reports - investment advisers are to make, keep, and furnish to the SEC copies of reports that the SEC deems necessary for the protection of investors. The records are subject to periodic, special, or other examinations by the SEC.
2. Section 204A - Prevention of misuse of nonpublic information -investment advisers are to establish, maintain, and enforce written policies and procedures designed to prevent the misuse in violation of the SEA.

Injunctions and prosecution of offenses (Section 21(d)) - if the SEC finds a person is engaged or about to be engaged in an action that would be a violation of the Act, the SEC can, via court action, file an injunction to prevent the act.

Civil penalties (Section 21A) - whenever the SEC finds a person has purchased or sold a security with knowledge of material non-public information, the SEC may, via court action, impose a civil penalty paid by the violator and the person who controlled the violator. The amount of penalty for the violator shall not exceed three times the profit gained or loss avoided, and the amount of penalty for the controlling person shall not exceed $1 million or three times the profit gained or loss avoided, whichever is greater.

SECTIONS 4 AND 5

Increases in criminal penalties - Section 4 of the Insider Trading and Securities Fraud Enforcement Act of 1988 increases criminal penalties found in Section 32(a) of the Securities Exchange Act of 1934 by amending it.

Securities Exchange Act of 1934 — Penalties (Section 32(a)) - a person who willfully violates a provision of the SEA can be fined up to $5 million and/or be imprisoned up to 20 years, except for if the person is not a natural person, then a fine can be imposed up to $25 million.

Liability to contemporaneous traders for insider trading (Section 5) - the Insider Trading and Securities Fraud Enforcement Act of 1988 adds Section 20A - Liability to contemporaneous traders for insider trading - to the Securities Exchange Act of 1934.

Liability to contemporaneous traders for insider trading (Section 20A) - a person who violates a provision of the SEA by performing a transaction deemed an insider trade is liable to any person who has contemporaneously transacted in the same security that is subject of the violation.

NASD Rule 2330

Authorization to Lend

A member is not to lend securities carried for the account of any customer unless the member has first obtained written authorization from the customer.

Segregation and Identification of Securities

A member is not to hold securities carried for the account of any customer that have been fully paid for unless the securities are segregated and identified as to the interest of the customer in the securities. Following are three popular ways of segregating customer's securities. In each, the date when the securities were segregated is to be noted.

1. Physical segregation by issue - with a list showing ownership of the securities.
2. Physical segregation by issue - affixing to each certificate, an identification with the name of the beneficial owner.
3. Specific segregation - of all certificates of each customer in separate envelopes.

General provisions - a member is to adhere to SEC rules in obtaining possession and control of securities, and in maintaining appropriate cash reserves.

Authorization to lend - a member is not to lend securities carried for the account of a customer that are eligible to be pledged or loaned unless the member has received written authorization from the customer to do so.

Segregation and identification of securities - a member is not to hold for the account of a customer, securities that have been fully paid for or which are excess margin securities, unless they are segregated and identified.

Brokerage Customers

The following are four types of potential brokerage customers:

- Individual customers - a single person.
- *Joint customers* - two or more persons sharing in the same account, usually relatives or business partners.
- *Corporate customers* - a customer that is a corporation.
- *Unincorporated associations* - groups of people that are not incorporated, such as partnerships, charitable organizations, schools, churches, hospitals, investment clubs, and hedge funds.

Fiduciaries

A fiduciary is someone who has the legal duty of acting on the behalf of another or the beneficiary. The fiduciary acts in the best interest of the beneficiary.

Prohibition regarding margin accounts and grants of trading authority to others - fiduciary accounts are prohibited from trading on margin. They are also prohibited from granting trading authority to others in many states.

Prudent man rules - a fiduciary must take actions that a prudent person would take, that is, act consistently with the investment objectives and in the best interest of the beneficiary. A fiduciary does not act in his own best interest.

Persons who are fiduciaries - administrators of estates, trustees, guardians, receivers in bankruptcy, committees or conservators for incompetents, and executors of estates.

WRAP ACCOUNTS, GIVE-UPS, AND PRIME BROKERS

Wrap accounts - a client account in which the brokerage is paid a fixed commission for a period of time, instead of a commission per transaction.

NYSE Rule 138 — Give-ups, which is when a broker executes a transaction for the benefit of another broker's client without replacing the client's broker in the relationship with the client, must be affected soon before, or soon after, the trade is executed.

Prime brokers - a broker who provides special services to certain clients such as hedge funds to be able to make leveraged trades and borrow securities.

COMPENSATION FOR UNDERWRITERS AND SYNDICATE MEMBERS

Underwriters and syndicate members typically get compensated from the underwriter's spread. The spread is the difference between the price at which the underwriter sells the security, and the price at which he purchased it from the issuer. There are three components of the spread - manager's fee, underwriter's fee, and concession.

1. Manager's fee - collected by only the syndicate manager.
2. Underwriter's fee - collected by all underwriters, including syndicate manager.
3. Concession - collected by non-syndicate member broker/dealers, as well as by the underwriters and syndicate manager.

Supervision of Retail and Institutional Customer-Related Activities

FINRA Rules 2010 and 2020

Standards of commercial honor and principles of trade (FINRA Rule 2010) - a member is to observe high standards of honor, and just and equitable principles of trade.

Use of manipulative, deceptive or other fraudulent devices (FINRA Rule 2020) - a member is prohibited from using any manipulative, deceptive, or fraudulent device in any transaction.

FINRA Rule 3310

Anti-money laundering compliance program - every member is to develop and implement an anti-money laundering program, approved by a senior manager in writing. This program shall at a minimum:

1. establish and implement policies and procedures to detect and cause required reporting of certain transactions
2. and implement policies, procedures, and controls to comply with the Bank Secrecy Act
3. provide for annual independent compliance testing by personnel
4. designate and identify to FINRA the individual(s) responsible for implementing and monitoring day-to-day operations and controls of the program
5. and provide ongoing training for personnel

Independent testing requirements (.01) - all members should take more frequent testing if circumstances warrant. Independent testing must be by a qualified designated person, and not by a person who performs the function being tested, a person designated as the anti-money laundering compliance person, or a person who reports to either.

Review of anti-money laundering compliance person information (.02) - each member must identify, review, and update information regarding its anti-money laundering compliance program

FINRA Rule 4512

Members are to maintain for each account the following information:

1. For all accounts - the customer's name and residence; whether or not the customer is of legal age; names of any associated persons responsible for the account; signature of the partner, officer, or manager signifying the account has been accepted according to policies and procedures; and for legal entity customers, the names of the persons authorized to transact on behalf of the entity.
2. For non-institutional accounts - the customer's tax ID or social security number; occupation of the customer with the name and address of employer; and whether the customer is an associated person of another member.
3. For discretionary accounts - any applicable information from above; record of the dated signature of each named natural authorized person.

NASD Rule 2340

NASD Rule 2340 - Customer account statements - members are to send an account statement at least once a quarter to customers that contains a description of any positions, money balances, or account activity, unless there has been none in the quarter. The account statement is to include a statement advising customers to promptly report any inaccuracies in the account statement.

DPP/REIT Securities - a member may provide an estimated per share value to the customer for direct participation programs (DPPs) or real estate investment trusts (REITs).

SEC RULE 17A-8

Financial recordkeeping and reporting of currency and foreign transactions (Rule 17a-8) - each registered broker or dealer subject to the Currency and Foreign Transactions Reporting Act of 1970 is to comply with the recordkeeping and record retention requirements of Chapter 10 of Title 31 of the Code of Federal Regulations. If Rule 17a-4 has requirements regarding the same records or reports but for different retention periods, the longer of the time requirements is to be kept.

REGULATION S-P

Limits on disclosure of nonpublic personal information to nonaffiliated third parties - nonpublic personal information may not be disclosed to nonaffiliated third parties unless the customer has been provided an initial notice, an opt out notice, and reasonable opportunity to opt out of the disclosure. The information may not be disclosed at all if the customer does opt out.

FINRA RULE 2210

Communications with the public (FINRA Rule 2210) - a qualified registered principal must approve all retail communication before its use or filing with FINRA, unless another member has already filed it and it has been approved and the member has not altered it. For institutional communications, members are to establish written procedures for review by a qualified registered principal of institutional communications. The procedures are to be designed to ensure that institutional communications company with the standards. All communications, retail and institutional, are to be retained according to requirements, and must include:

1. a copy of the communication
2. the name of any registered principal approving of the communication
3. if not approved by a registered principal prior to first use, the name of the person who prepared it
4. information about the source of information used in graphic illustrations
5. if approval is not required for retail communication, the name of the member that filed it with FINRA, as well as the letter from FINRA

Filing requirements and review procedures - for 1 year after becoming a member with FINRA, a member must submit to FINRA all published retail communication at least ten days prior to publication. Various types of retail communications are to be filled at least ten days prior to publication, or within ten days of first use, depending on the type of communication. FINRA may submit member communications to a spot-check, under which the member is to submit to FINRA information requested regarding a communication.

CONTENT STANDARDS

1. All member communications are to be based in fair dealing and good faith. They must be fair, balanced, and provide a sound basis for evaluating facts.
2. It is prohibited to make false, exaggerated, unwarranted, promissory, or misleading statements.
3. Information can only be based in a footnote if the placement does not inhibit the readers understanding of the information.

4. Statements are to be clear and not misleading in the context in which they are made.
5. Members must consider the nature of the audience and are to provide details and explanations when appropriate.
6. Communications cannot predict or project performance, imply that past performance will recur, or make exaggerated or unwarranted claims.

IM-2210-2

Communications with the public about variable life insurance and variable annuities - in addition to the standards in FINRA Rule 2210, additional guidelines must be met regarding communications with the public about variable life insurance and variable annuities. All communications must clearly describe the product as a variable annuity or life insurance policy. There is to be no representation that the investments are short term, and all references to liquidity must include clear language that describes the negative aspects of early redemption. The relative safety of guarantee must not be overemphasized, and there can be no representation that a guarantee applies to the investment return or value of the account.

FINRA RULE 2216

Collateralized mortgage obligations - a collateralized mortgage obligation is a multi-class debt instrument backed by a pool of mortgage pass-through securities or mortgage loans.

1. Disclosure standards - all communications regarding CMOs:
   a. must include the name of the product - "Collateralized Mortgage Obligation";
   b. is not to compare CMOs to any other type of investment;
   c. must disclose that any government backing applies only to the principle and not the premium paid; and
   d. must disclose that the yield and average life will fluctuate.
2. Required educational material - a member must offer to a potential customer, educational materials regarding the product that includes a discussion of the characteristics and risks of CMOs, the structure of a CMO, and the relationship between mortgage loans and mortgage securities. It should also include questions an investor should ask and a glossary of terms.
3. Promotion of specific CMOs - retail communications that relay yield information or promote a specific security are to comply with additional standards.

FINRA RULE 3230

No person associated with a member is to make an outbound phone call to:

1. any residence before 8 AM or after 9 PM unless there is an established business relationship, there has been an invitation to do so, or the person being called is a broker or dealer
2. any person registered on the FTC national do not call list, unless there is an existing business relationship, prior express written consent, or a personal relationship

Safe harbor provision - a person will not be in violation of the telemarketing rules if the act was a mistake and usual business practices follow the standards.

Procedures - prior to engaging in telemarketing, a member must institute a procedure to comply with the rules. There must be a written policy, training of personnel, recording and disclosure of do-not-call requests, identification of sellers and telemarketers, and maintenance of do-not-call lists. A person's request to not be called is to apply to the individual making the call, not affiliated persons or entities unless is it reasonable to assume such.

Selected other provisions - if outsourced telemarketing is used, the member is responsible for making sure the rules are followed. A telemarketer cannot have caller identification blocked. If an automated dialer is used the phone call cannot be "abandoned," or in other words, the person who answers cannot be left unconnected to a person for longer than two seconds.

SEC Rule 156

It is prohibited for any person to use misleading sales literature. Sales literature is misleading if it contains any untrue statements of material facts or omits to state a material fact. In determining whether or not a statement is misleading, weight should be given to pertinent factors regarding context including but not limited to:

1. a statement could be misleading because of:
   a. other statements made in connection
   b. the absence of explanation, qualifications, limitation, or other statements
   c. general economic of financial conditions or circumstances
   d. representations about past of future performance could be misleading because of the situation

FINRA Rules 2090 and 2111

Know your customer (FINRA Rule 2090) - members of FINRA are to use reasonable diligence when opening and maintaining accounts for customers, and to get to know essential facts about the customer and concerning the authority of each person acting on behalf of a customer.

Suitability (FINRA Rule 2111) - a member must have a reasonable basis to believe that an investment or strategy is suitable for the customer based on the information the member has gained, according to the "know your customer" rule. Pertinent information includes the customer's age, other investments, financial situation, tax status, objectives, experience, investment time horizon, liquidity needs, and risk tolerance. For an institutional customer, the member is to have reasonable belief the customer is capable of evaluating risks and has indicated that it is exercising independent judgment.

FINRA Rule 2114

No member is to recommend a customer purchase or sell short any OTC equity security, unless the member has reviewed the current financial statements and material business information of the issuer and determined that the information provides a reasonable basis. The registered person designated to make this review is to be a General Securities Principal or General Securities Sales Supervisor with appropriate skills, background, and knowledge. If the issue has not met any of its necessary filing requirements, the review is to include inquiry about the circumstances of the failure to file, and any subsequent recommendation to a customer is to be in writing.

FINRA Rule 2124

Net transactions with customers (FINRA Rule 2124) - a member executing a net transaction with a customer must first disclose it and obtain consent from the customer. A net transaction is a when a member, after receiving an order from a customer, purchases the security at a different price and subsequently sells it to the customer to fulfill the original order, keeping the proceeds that make up the difference in price.

FINRA Rule 2130

Approval procedures for day-trading accounts (FINRA Rule 2130) - a day-trading member may not open an account for a non-institutional customer without furnishing to the customer a risk disclosure statement and without having approved the customer's account for day trading according to certain criteria. In lieu of approving the customer's account, the member can obtain a written agreement from the customer stating the customer does not intend the account to use for day-trading activities.

SIPC RULES 100, 101, 102

The purpose of these Rules are to determine what accounts held by a person with a SIPC member are deemed to be accounts held in a capacity other than his individual capacity. Accounts under different capacities are separate customers.

Individual accounts - accounts held in a person's own name is an individual account, and multiples of such accounts of the same person are to be combined and considered single accounts of a separate customer.

Accounts held by executors or administrators - an account in the name of a decedent, a decedent's estate, or an executor or administrator of such. Multiples of such accounts of the same person are to be combined and considered single accounts of a separate customer.

FINRA RULE 2270

Day Trading Risk Disclosure Statement (FINRA Rule 2270) - in addition to providing the customer with the risk disclosure statement, the member must post the same disclosure on the member's website. The risks disclosures include: day trading is extremely risky; be cautious of claims of large profits from day trading; day trading requires knowledge of securities markets; day trading requires knowledge of a firm's operations; day trading will generate substantial commissions, even if the per trade cost is low; day trading on margin or short selling may result in losses beyond your initial investment; and potential registration requirements.

FINRA RULES 5230, 2251, AND 2267

Payments involving publications that influence the market price of a security (FINRA Rule 5230) - a member is not to give anything of value to a person in order to influence or reward an action related to a publication or other media.

Forwarding of proxy and other materials (FINRA Rule 2251) - a member is to forward promptly all information required by this Rule and the SEC regarding a security to its beneficial owner if the name of registration is different than the name of the beneficial owner.

Investor education and protection (FINRA Rule 2267) - a member is to annually provide in writing to every customer the FINRA BrokerCheck Hotline number, the FINRA web-site address, and a statement informing the customer of an available BrokerCheck brochure.

FINRA RULE 2264

All FINRA members must provide to any non-institutional customers opening a margin account, a margin disclosure statement in written or electronic form before or at the time of opening the account. The disclosure is also required to be delivered to each margin customer annually. If customers are able to open an account on the internet, the disclosure statement is to be posted on the website in a clear a conspicuous manner. The statement is provided in FINRA Rule 2264 and makes various statements warning customers of risk.

RISK STATEMENTS
- You can lose more funds than you deposit in the margin account.
- The firm can force the sale of securities or other assets in your account(s).

- The firm can sell your securities or other assets without contacting you.
- You are not entitled to choose which securities or other assets in your account(s) are liquidated or sold to meet a margin call.
- The firm can increase its "house" maintenance margin requirements at any time and is not required to provide you advance written notice.
- You are not entitled to an extension of time on a margin call.

FINRA RULE 4210

Basket — a group of stocks eligible to be executed in a single trade.

Designated account — an account of certain banks, investment companies, insurance companies, state or political subdivisions, or pension plans.

Margin — the necessary amount of equity to be maintained for a security position in an account.

Major foreign sovereign debt — a debt security issued by a foreign entity that has debt securities that are subordinated in relation and the security has been ranked in the top rating category by a nationally recognized rating organization.

Exempt account — any member or registered broker-dealer, or certain persons with a net worth of $45 million or more.

Other marginable non-equity securities — includes certain debt securities that are not traded on a national exchange and certain private pass-through securities.

Initial margin - the required opening deposit in a margin account.

Maintenance margin - the required margin which must be maintained in an account, calculated as:

1. 25% of the current market value of securities
2. the greater of $2.50 per share or 100% or the current market value for any stock short positions of stock trading at less than $5 per share
3. the greater of $5 per share or 100% or the current market value for any stock short positions of stock trading at more than $5 per share
4. the greater of $5 per share or 30% of the current market value for each bond short position
5. 20% of the current market value for any security futures contracts
6. 100% of the current market value for non-margin eligible securities held "long"

Additional margin - a procedure must be in place for members to review type and limit of credit extended, to formulate their own margin requirements, and to review the need for instituting higher margin requirements.

Exceptions to rule for offsetting long and short positions - if a security in "long" position is exchangeable or convertible into a security in "short" position, the margin required is 10% of current market value of the "long" security. If the "long" and "short" are for the same security, the margin required is 5%.

Exempted securities - net "long" and "short" positions in obligations that are guaranteed by the United States or that are highly rated foreign sovereign debt securities are exempted and given their own margin requirements. "Long" and "short" positions in exempted securities other than United States obligations shall maintain a margin of 7% of the current market value.

Non-equity securities - "long" and "short" positions in non-equity securities are to maintain a margin of 10% of the current market value for investment grade securities, and the greater of 20% of the current market value or 7% of the principal for other non-equity securities.

Baskets - a member can make basket transactions for a registered market maker based on a margin determined to be adequate by the concerned parties.

Specialists' and market makers' accounts - a member can have a margin account for an approved market maker based on a margin determined to be adequate by the concerned parties.

Broker-dealer accounts - a member can have a proprietary margin account for another broker-dealer based on a margin determined to be adequate by the concerned parties.

Shelf-registered and other control and restricted securities - securities that are part of a continuous or delayed offering (shelf-registered securities) are subject to the same maintenance requirements as other securities. For other control and restricted securities, the margin to be maintained is 40% of the current market value for "long" securities.

Determination of value for margin purposes - to determine required margin, all national exchange securities are to be valued at current market prices.

"When issued" and "when distributed" securities - the margin required for "when issued" securities is the same as if the securities were issued. If in a cash account, the margin required to be maintained is the same as if it were a margin account.

Guaranteed accounts - an account guaranteed by another account can be consolidated with such account, and the margin can be calculated based on the aggregate position, provided the guarantee is in writing.

Consolidation of accounts - if customer accounts are consolidated, the margin can be calculated on the aggregate position of the two accounts, provided the customer has consented.

Time within which margin or "mark to market" must be obtained - the amount of margin or "mark to market" required must be obtained as quickly as possible, and never more than 15 business days after the deficiency date.

Practice of meeting Regulation T margin calls by liquidation prohibited - members are not to allow customers to defer the cash deposit required by a margin call or to make a practice of liquidating a commitment in the account to satisfy the call.

Special initial and maintenance margin requirements:

1. FINRA reserves the right to prescribe higher initial margin requirements, higher maintenance margin requirements, and other terms and conditions.
2. Special requirements for pattern day traders - the minimum margin required for a pattern day trader is $25,000, and he cannot trade in excess of his day-trading buying power, which is his equity at of the close of the previous business day, less any margin requirement.

Free-riding in cash accounts prohibited - in a cash account a customer may not make a practice of making transaction where the cost of the securities purchased is met by the sale of the same securities. Additionally, a customer may not sell securities in a cash account which are to be received against payment from another broker-dealer where the securities were purchased but not yet paid for.

Portfolio margin - if a member so chooses, instead of using the margin requirements set forth, a member can require a portfolio margin for certain customers, which is a method of determining margin requirements based on specific account monitoring requirements and SEC approved theoretical pricing models.

RULE 4210(F)(8)(B)

Pattern day trader — a customer who executes four or more trades within five business days, unless those trades represent 6% or less of the customer's total trades.

Day-trading buying power — the equity the day-trading customer has in their account less any maintenance margin, multiplied by four (for equity securities).

Special requirements for pattern day traders — the special requirements for pattern day traders include:

1. a minimum equity requirement of $25,000
2. they cannot trade in excess of their day-trading buying power
3. if a pattern day trader fails to meet maintenance margin calls as required, they will be permitted only to trade on a cash available basis for 90 days or until the margin call is met
4. minimum equity funds deposited cannot be withdrawn for a minimum of two business days after deposit

FINRA RULES 2268 AND 4514

Requirements when using predispute arbitration agreements with customers (FINRA 2268) - any predispute arbitration clause is to be highlighted and to be accompanied by a statement with specific disclosure as to what the customer is agreeing to.

Negotiable instruments drawn from a customer's account (FINRA Rule 4514) - no member may obtain or write a check or other negotiable instrument on the account of a customer without written authorization from the customer. This written documentation, if separate from the actual negotiable instrument, is to be kept for at least three years.

NASD RULE 2410

Net prices to persons not in investment banking or securities business (NASD Rule 2410) - no member is to offer a security or to confirm a purchase or sale of a security from any person not involved in investment banking or securities business using a price that has a concession, discount or allowance. All such transactions are to be in a net dollar or basis price.

NASD RULE 2420

Transactions with non-members - a member is not to deal with a non-member broker or dealer with prices, fees, or commissions different than those given to the general public.

Transactions with foreign non-members - these rules are not applicable to foreign non-members. If a member deals with a foreign non-member with a concession, discount, or other allowance, the member shall require an agreement and the foreign non-member will comply with these rules if selling to purchasers in the United States.

Definition of non-member broker or dealer - a broker or dealer who conducts interstate commerce but is not registered with the Commission.

Transactions between members and non-members (IM-2420-1)

1. Certain non-members of the Association are: persons excluded from the definition of member in Rule 0120, expelled dealers, suspended dealers, broker or dealer with registration revoked by the SEC, and a broker or dealer with membership cancelled or resigned.
2. Exempted securities/transactions - the Rule does not apply to exempted securities defined in Section 3(a)(12) of the Act. The Rule does not apply to transactions enacted on an exchange.
3. Over-the-counter transactions in securities other than exempted securities - a member is not to participate in a selling group with a non-member to acquire and distribute an issue of securities. If a member is participating as part of a selling group, the member is not to allow any selling concession or discount to a bank or trust company. A member may not participate in a selling group with a suspended or expelled dealer.

Continuing commission policy (IM-2420-2) - payment of continuing commission is allowed, as long as the commission is being received by a member. If such person ceases to become a member, the payments must stop.

NASD RULE 2510

Excessive transactions - when a member has discretionary powers over the account of a customer, the member may not transact purchases or sales that are in excessive size or frequency in comparison to the size and character of the account.

Authorization and acceptance of account - a member may not exercise its own discretion in a customer's account unless they have received written authorization from the customer.

Approval and review of transactions - a member shall quickly and in writing approve all discretionary transactions and regularly review all discretionary accounts to prevent any excessive transactions.

Exceptions - the Rule does not apply to the time and price that an order received from the customer is executed at, though such orders are only valid through the end of the business day. It also does not apply to certain bulk exchanges of net asset value of money market mutual funds.

NASD RULE 3110(I) AND FINRA RULES 4515 AND 3250

Holding of customer mail (NASD Rule 3110(i)) - upon a customer's instructions, a member can hold mail for the customer for up to two months when the customer is on vacation or traveling, and up to three months if the customer is going abroad.

Changes in account name or designation (FINRA Rule 4515) - any change in a customer account name or designation must be approved by a qualified and registered principal designated by the member who is to be informed of the facts relating to the change. Approval needs to be in writing.

Designation of accounts (FINRA Rule 3250) - a member may not hold an account on its books in a name other than the name of the customer, except for a number or symbol designation for which the customer has signed a document attesting to ownership of the account.

SEC RULE 10B-10 AND FINRA RULE 2232

Confirmation of transactions (SEC Rule 10b-10) - broker/dealers must disclose certain information to the customer in writing at or before the completion of a transaction. This disclosure must contain specific information including the date and time of the transaction; the identity, price, and number of shares; agency disclosure of the broker/dealer; disclosure of any odd-lot differential fee paid for by the customer; and certain other disclosures for debt securities. There are some exceptions to the Rule such as certain transactions that are part of an investment company plan.

Customer confirmations (FINRA Rule 2232) - a member is to send to the customer a written notification at or before the completion of a transaction.

SEC Rule 15c1-7

When a broker/dealer has discretionary powers over the account of a customer, the broker/dealer may not transact purchases or sales that are in excessive size or frequency in comparison to the size and character of the account.

When a broker/dealer has discretionary powers over the account of a customer, the broker/dealer must, immediately after completing the transaction, record the name of the customer, the name, amount and price of the security, and the date and time of the transaction.

Customer Information Documentation and Supplementary Documentation

Customer information data

1. Customer identification data.
2. Name and occupation of third party authorized to act on behalf of the beneficial owner. The types of authorization could be limited authorization, full authorization, and discretionary powers to broker-dealers.
3. Payment/delivery and/or duplicate mailing instructions which include: transfer and ship, hold in "street name," transfer and hold in safekeeping, hold cash or forward cash balance on settlement date, deliver against payment to a bank or depository, and reinvestment plan (reinvesting cash balances).
4. Signature and acceptance of account by general securities or options principal of firm.

Supplementary documentation - hypothecation agreement; loan consent agreement; credit agreement; powers of attorney - discretionary accounts; options agreement; arbitration agreement; account guarantee acknowledgment; and W-8 and W-9 tax withholding forms.

Supervision of Trading and Market Making Activities

NASD IM-2110-3 AND FINRA RULE 5280

Front running policy (NASD IM-2110-3) - a person who has material, non-public information regarding an imminent block transaction of an underlying security may not buy or sell an option or security future in that security for their benefit or for the benefit of an associated person. A person who has material, non-public information regarding an imminent block transaction in an option or security future may not buy or sell the underlying security for their benefit or for the benefit of an associated person.

Trading ahead of research reports (FINRA Rule 5280) - members may not establish, decrease, increase or liquidate an inventory position in a security based on advanced non-public information of the content of a research report.

FINRA RULES 5210, 5220, AND 5290

Publication of transactions and quotations (Rule 5210) - no member shall publish communication about a purchase, sale, or quote unless the member believes it was bona fide.

Offers at stated prices (Rule 5220) - a member may not make an offer unless they are prepared to transact at that price. Though sometimes "backing-away" is constituted, regularly "backing-away" puts into question the validity of the dealer's quotes and disrupts the course of regular business.

Order entry and execution practices (Rule 5290) - an order cannot be split up into smaller orders simply for the purpose of increasing commissions or payments.

FINRA RULES 5260, 6120, AND 6121

Prohibition on transactions, publication of quotations, or publication of indications of interest during trading halts (FINRA Rule 5260) - if trading is halted for a specific security, no trading activities can be made on the security.

Trading halts (FINRA Rule 6120) - FINRA will halt the trading of a security otherwise than on an exchange in certain situations when the market in power calls for a trading halt, or to permit dissemination of material news, obtain material information, obtain material information in the public interest. Other reasons include when extraordinary market activity is occurring.

Trading halts due to extraordinary market volatility (FINRA Rule 6121) - FINRA will halt all trading activity otherwise than on an exchange in any stock if other major securities markets have done the same in response to extraordinary market volatility, or if directed by the SEC.

FINRA RULES 5310, 6438, AND 6430

Best execution and interpositioning (Rule 5310) - a member must use due diligence in ensuring that the transaction is made on the market best for the security so the price to the customer is favorable. Additionally, a member cannot put a 3rd party between himself and the best market, unless there is an acceptable circumstance.

Displaying priced quotations in multiple quotation mediums (Rule 6438) - if a member displays quotes on multiple real-time quotation mediums, the same priced quotes for a security are to be displayed in each medium.

Recording of quotation information (Rule 6430) - any OTC market maker that displays real-time quotes must keep record of certain information including the submitting firm, inter-dealer quotation system, trade date, time quote displayed, security name and symbol, bid and bid quote size, offer and offer quote size, prevailing inside bid, and prevailing inside offer.

FINRA RULE 5320

Prohibition against trading ahead of customer orders (FINRA Rule 5320) - a member that accepts an order from a customer and does not immediately execute it is prohibited from trading that same security on the same side of the market for its own account at a price that would satisfy the customer's order unless the member immediately after executes the customer order at the same or better price.

ADF AND FINRA RULES 6230, 6240, AND 6220

Alternative Display Facility (ADF) Data Systems - an ADF is an alternative system for displaying quote and trade information. FINRA reserves the right to test an Alternative Display Facility for whatever studies are necessary (Rule 6230).

Prohibition from locking or crossing quotations in NMS stocks (Rule 6240) - members are not to make a practice of displaying quotes that lock or cross a protected quotation.

Definitions (Rule 6220)

1. Certification record - the document with which an ADF trading center must comply to display its quotes through the ADF.
2. CQS security - a security eligible for the Consolidated Quotation Plan.
3. Normal unit of trading - 100 shares of the security, unless otherwise determined.
4. Registered reporting ADF ECN - a FINRA ECN member that displays on an ADF.
5. Stop stock price - the price that a stop stock transaction is executed.
6. Stop stock transaction - a transaction where the parties agree to execute at a specific price or better.

FINRA RULES 5250 AND 6250

Payments for market making (FINRA Rule 5250) - a member may not receive payment from an issuer of a security in exchange for publishing a quote or acting as a market maker in a security.

Quote and order access requirements (FINRA Rule 6250) - an ADF trading center, for each security displays a bid and/or offer, must provide other ADF trading centers direct electronic access. This access is to include access for broker-dealers that are not ADF trading centers. The ADF trading center is required to keep certain information for each order they receive to include a unique order identifier; order entry firm; order side; order quantity; issue identifier; order price; order negotiable flag; time in force; order date; order time; minimal acceptable quantity; market making firm; and trade-or-move flag.

FINRA RULES 6271, 6275, AND 6140

Registration as an ADF market maker or an ADF ECN (FINRA Rule 6271) - quotes in ADF-eligible securities can only be entered by ADF market makers or ADF ECNs. A FINRA member who desires to be an ADF market maker or ADF ECN must apply to FINRA.

Withdrawal of quotations (FINRA Rule 6275) - an ADF trading center that desires to withdraw its quotations in a security must contact ADF Operations to get an excused withdrawal status. If an ADF trading center is unable to immediately or automatically respond to orders, it must immediately withdraw its quotes and contact ADF Operations. Excused withdrawal status is granted based on certain conditions.

Other trading practices (FINRA Rule 6140) - no member shall purchase NMS stock at higher or lower prices with the intent to create an appearance of activity in a security and establishing a false price. No member can profit from false or misleading trading activity.

FINRA RULES 6273 AND 2265

Normal business hours (FINRA Rule 6273) - an ADF trading center is to open at 9:30 AM Eastern Time and close no earlier than 4:00 PM Eastern Time.

Extended hours trading risk disclosure (FINRA Rule 2265) - if a member is to permit a customer to trade in hours passed normal business hours, a disclosure of extended hours trading risks is to be furnished to the customer. These risks include lower liquidity, higher volatility, changing prices, unlinked markets, news announcements, and wider spreads.

FINRA RULE 6320A

Designated securities — NMS stocks defined in Rule 600(b)(47).

Normal market hours — 9:30 AM Eastern Time to 4:00 PM Eastern Time.

Normal unit of trading — 100 shares, unless otherwise determined.

Otherwise than on an exchange — a transaction that takes place somewhere else than on a national exchange.

Round lot holder — any holder of a normal unit of trading.

Stop stock price — the price at which a stop stock transaction will be executed.

Stop stock transaction — a transaction that executes at a stop stock price or better.

*Terms defined here are to have the same meaning as in FINRA by-*laws and rules; Rule 600 of Regulation NMS; and the Joint Self-Regulatory Organization Plan Governing the Collection, Consolidation, and Dissemination of Quotation and Transaction Information for NASDAQ-Listed Securities Traded on Exchanges on an Unlisted Trading Privilege Basis, unless otherwise defined.

FINRA RULES 6281 AND 6380B

Transactions otherwise than on an exchange - transactions conducted by FINRA members otherwise than on an exchange must be reported to ADR TRACS, FINRAs Trade Reporting and Comparison Service.

When transactions are reported - transactions by trade reporting facility participants are to report the transaction within 10 seconds after execution. Members are to timestamp all trade tickets upon execution.

Who reports - if between two members, the executing party will report the transaction. If between a member and non-member, the member will report the transaction.

What information is reported - stock symbol; number of units; price; whether it is a buy, sell or cross, sell short, or sell short exempt; time of execution; and an order identifier.

FINRA Rule 6440 and NASDAQ Rule 4121

Trading and quotation halt in OTC equity securities (FINRA Rule 6440) - if it is necessary to protect investors, FINRA may direct members to halt trading in an OTC equity security in certain instances such as if the security is an OTC ADR and the foreign market has halted trading in the security, or if an extraordinary event has occurred that deems a halt necessary.

NASDAQ market closing (NASDAQ Rule 4121) — NASDAQ will, upon SEC request, close the market, or halt all trading, in the case of extraordinary activity.

FINRA Rule 6500

Applicability (FINRA Rule 6510) - the rules in FINRA Rule 6500 are known as the OTC Bulletin Board Rules. They regulate the use of the OTC Bulletin Board by broker-dealer members of FINRA.

Operation of the service (FINRA Rule 6520) - the OTCBB is an electronic quote service. Market makers enter their quotes in individual securities, real-time. Quotes can be the price of bids/offers, unpriced indications of interest, or bids/offers with a modifier reflecting unsolicited customer interest. Market makers can access the quotes of others including the highest bid and lowest offer in OTCBB-eligible securities that have at least two market makers displaying two-sided markets.

OTCBB-eligible securities (FINRA Rule 6530):

1. Certain domestic equity securities that are not listed on a national exchange.
2. Certain American Depository Receipts (ADRs).
3. Certain equity securities that are delisting from a national exchange or are subject to a suspension from a national exchange.
4. Certain Direct Participation Programs.

FINRA Rule 6540

Permissible quotation entries - market makers can enter one-sided quotes for OTCBB-eligible securities - orders that reflect unsolicited customer interest.

Impermissible quotation entries - one-sided quotes cannot be entered if they do not satisfy requirements in Rule 6530.

Voluntary termination of registration - a market maker can voluntarily terminate its registration of an OTCBB-eligible security by removing its quotes for that security from the service.

More than one trading location -if a market maker trades in more than 1 location, a fifth character is to be added to its identifier for the security, identifying the geographic location.

Clearance and settlement - market makers are to have their transactions of OTCBB securities cleared through a registered clearing agency that uses a continuous net settlement system.

SIPC 100 Series

Accounts held by a corporation, partnership, or unincorporated association - accounts of a corporation are to be separate from any accounts of a person owning said corporation.

Trust accounts - a trust account is a qualifying trust account if it is held on behalf of a valid and subsisting express trust created by a written instrument.

Joint accounts - a joint account is a qualifying joint account if it is owned jointly, whether it by with the right of survivorship, tenants in common, or marital community property, as long as each co-owner has authority to act in regards to the entirety of the account.

Prohibited acts - failure to pay assessment or file reports; engaging in business after appointment of trustee or initiation of direct payment procedure; and concealment of assets; false statements or claims.

SIPC logo - every member of SIPC is to display the SIPC logo continuously in a prominent location.

SEA RULE 10B5-1

Trading "on the basis of" material nonpublic information in insider trading (SEA Rule 10b5-1) - a person is deemed to be trading on the basis of material nonpublic information if the person was aware of the information at the time of the transaction unless:

1. he became aware of the information after entering into an agreement to transact;
2. he instructed another to transact prior to becoming aware of the information;
3. he adopted a written plan for trading securities before becoming aware of the information.

SEC RULES 15C2-7 AND 15C2-11

Identification of quotations (Rule 15c2-7) - when a quote is submitted, the inter-dealer quotation system must be informed and must disclose each published quotation. If two broker-dealers enter into an arrangement to each enter certain quotations for a security, it must be disclosed to all broker-dealers with similar quotations.

Initiation or resumption of quotations with specified information (Rule 15c2-11) - in order to publish a quote, a broker-dealer must have certain documents or information regarding the security. These documents or information can include a copy of the prospectus, a copy of the offering circular, or a copy of the issuer's most recent annual report.

LENDER'S PRIVILEGES IN REGARDS TO SHORT SALES

Return of securities - a broker has the right to call away, or force the customer to return, the securities lent to him for a short sale.

Marking to the market - the process of a broker changing the value of an asset, such as stocks, to the current market value. This is done regularly in margin accounts to determine if the appropriate level of equity is being maintained in the account.

Dividends and rights - any dividends or rights received during the short sale process are paid by the customer to the lender.

Voting rights - are not held by the short seller; they stay with the holder of record. When the short seller sells the shares short on the market, the voting rights go with the shares to the purchaser.

SEC RULE 15C6-1 AND FINRA RULES 6274 AND 6350

Settlement cycle (SEC Rule 15c6-1) - a broker or dealer is not to enter into a transaction calling for settlement beyond the 3rd business day after execution unless both parties expressly agree to it. This rule does not apply to certain contracts for purchase or sale of limited partnership interests not listed on an exchange or for purchase or sale of securities the SEC exempts from the Rule. The Rule also does not apply in certain situations where the pricing of the security happens after 4:30 PM Eastern Time and sold by an issuer to an underwriter.

FINRA rules regarding clearance and settlement (FINRA Rules 6274 and 6350) - members must clear and settle transactions with a clearing agency that uses a continuous net settlement system.

CLEARING AND SETTLEMENT IN BROKER-TO-BROKER TRANSACTIONS

In broker-to-broker transactions, the two sides of a trade are matched in the exchange, or "locked-in", and then sent to a clearing agency for clearing and settling the transaction. Clearing companies perform netting of trades for broker-to-broker transactions. A clearing agency receives a large number of transactions needing settling per day, and netting reduces the number of the transactions that actually need financial settlement. Continuous Net Settlement is an automated system that centralizes the settlement of compared transactions, and maintains flow. After the clearing agency has settled the security positions, the broker's settling banks settle any money positions.

CLEARING CORPORATIONS

Securities firms have to be a member of one of four clearing corporations: National Securities Clearing Corporation, Midwest Clearing Corporation, Philadelphia Clearing Corporation, Pacific Clearing Corporation.

DEPOSITORY TRUST AND CLEARING CORPORATIONS

The Depository Trust and Clearing Corporations is a clearing agency that clears and settles trades for broker-to-broker transactions through its subsidiary the National Securities Clearing Corporation (NSCC). The Depository Trust and Clearing Corporations provide for securities certificate safekeeping by making all transfers of ownership via electronic transactions.

FINRA RULE 11100

Scope of the Uniform Practice Code (FINRA Rule 11100) - the Uniform Practice Code covers all over-the-counter secondary market securities' transactions, except for transaction between members that are cleared through a registered clearing agency, certain transactions otherwise exempted by the SEA of 1934, certain transaction of investment companies, and certain direct participation program transactions.

FINRA RULE 11120

Committee - the UPC Committee that administers the Code.

Delivery date - settlement date.

Ex-date - the date on and after which a security is traded without a specific dividend or distribution.

Immediate return receipt - an acknowledgement by the recipient of a written notice which is sent upon receipt of the notice the same media.

Record date - the date used to determine the holder of a security who is entitled to receive dividends, interest, or principal payments.

Trade date - if a bid or offer is accepted in a later time zone that it was originated, the trade date is to be the day of the later time zone.

FINRA RULE 11130

Each party to a transaction is to send a "when, as and if issued" or "when as and if distributed" confirmation or comparison which is to include a description of the security, a designation of FINRA as the authority, and a provision for marking the contract to market. All "when, as and if issued" or

"when as and if distributed" contracts are to be "and accrued interest" to date of settlement - meaning to include any interest accrued up to the date of the transaction settlement. Since the issuance or distribution can be long delayed, the contracts are to be market-to-market.

FINRA Rule 11140

Other than cash transactions, all transactions are "ex-dividend," ex-rights," or "ex-warrants" on the day specified by the Committee or by the applicable national securities exchange. Normally, the ex-date is to be the 2nd day prior to the record date for cash dividends or distributions that are less than 25% of the value of the security. The ex-date shall be one day prior to the record date for cash dividends or distributions in excess of 25% of the value of the security. For rights, the ex-date is the first business day after the effective date of the registration statement. If information is received late regarding any ex-dates, the ex-date will be on the first business day practical as deemed by the Committee.

FINRA Rules 11150, 11160, and 11170

Transactions "ex-Interest" in bonds which are dealt in "flat" (FINRA Rule 11150) - all bonds or similar evidences of indebtedness, except for cash transactions, are to be traded "ex-interest" on the second business day prior to the record date. If information is received late, the ex-date is to be on the first day practical as determined by the Committee.

"Ex-liquidating payments" (FINRA Rule 11160) - all stocks, and bonds or similar evidences of indebtedness are to be traded "ex-liquidating payments."

Transactions in "part-redeemed" bonds (FINRA Rule 11170) - in a transaction of a bond that has been partially redeemed, the settlement price is determined by multiplying the contract price by the original principal amount.

FINRA Rules 11190 and 11200

Reconfirmation and pricing service participants (FINRA Rule 11190) - members are to participate in fail reconfirmation and pricing services when offered for clearing over-the-counter securities transactions.

Comparisons or confirmations and "don't know notices" (FINRA Rule 11200) - each party to a transaction is to send a comparison or confirmation of the transaction no later than the first business day following the transaction. The same shall be sent on the same day for cash transactions. If any discrepancies exist, a correction is to be sent to the party in error. A properly executed Uniform Comparison or Confirmation is to be used for these purposes. If a party to a transaction by the 4th business day following a transaction does not receive a comparison, confirmation, or signed "don't know notice" in return, there are specific procedures to be followed.

FINRA Rule 11220

Confirmations and comparisons are to include an adequate description of the security as well as the price at which the transaction was made and any other necessary information.

FINRA Rule 11320

Cash - for a cash transaction, delivery is on the day of the transaction.

Regular way - for a "regular way" transaction, delivery is to be not before the third business day after the transaction.

Seller's option - for a transaction in which the seller has an option, delivery is to be on the date the option expires or on the third business day after the transaction.

Buyer's option - for a transaction in which the buyer has an option, deliver is to be on the date the option expires.

Contracts due on holidays or Saturdays - contracts due on days that are not business days are to be due on the next business day.

Delayed delivery - if a transaction is for delayed delivery, delivery is to be on the specified date and time.

Prior to delivery date - if a seller delivers prior to any date specified in the rules, the purchaser has the discretion whether or not to accept.

Time and place of delivery - delivery is to be made at the office of the purchaser and between the hours established by rule or practice in the community.

FINRA RULES 11361, 11362, 11363, AND 11364

Units of delivery — stocks (FINRA Rule 11361) - stock certificates delivered for settlement can be on one certificate if for 100 shares or exact multiples of 100. If for more than 100 shares but not a multiple of 100, it is to be in multiples of 100 and then the amount of the odd-lot separately.

Units of delivery — bonds (FINRA Rule 11362) - bonds to be delivered in coupon bearer form are to be in denominations of $1,000 or in denominations $100 or multiples thereof. For registered bonds are to be in denominations of $1,000 or in denominations of $100 or multiples thereof, not to exceed denominations of $100,000.

Units of delivery — unit investment trust securities (FINRA Rule 11363) - the minimum delivery unit for a unit investment trust is a single unit of the trust.

Units of delivery — certificates of deposit for bonds (FINRA Rule 113640) - the minimum delivery unit for certificates of deposit for bonds is the same as in Rule 11362.

FINRA RULES 11410 AND 11520

Delivery of securities with draft attached (FINRA Rule 11410)

1. Time of presentation - if a draft accompanies the delivery of a security, the draft only needs to be accepted on a business day and between normal business hours. At anything other time, the drawee has the option.
2. Prior to settlement date - any acceptance of a draft prior to the settlement date is the option of the drawee.
3. With irregularities - any acceptance of a draft with irregularities is the option of the drawee.

Delivery of mutilated securities (FINRA Rule 11520) - a mutilated security - one which contains material information that cannot be discerned - is not properly delivered until authenticated.

FINRA RULES 11550 AND 11574 AND NYSE RULE 200

Assignments and powers of substitution; delivery of registered securities (FINRA Rule 11550) - in order for a registered security to be properly delivered it must have with it an assignment and powers of substitution.

National medallion signature guarantee program (NYSE Rule 200) - a member or clearing agency can assign and register securities subject to a settlement by using a medallion stamp on the security. This medallion signifies delivery when it executes an assignment.

Certificate in name of deceased person, trustee, etc. (FINRA Rule 11574) - a delivery is not a good delivery if the assignment of power of substitution was executed by a person since deceased, a trustee, a guardian, an infant, executor, administrator, receiver in bankruptcy, agent, attorney, or with a qualification, restriction, or special designation. Exceptions are domestic individual executors, domestic individual trustees under an inter vivos or testamentary trust, and domestic guardians.

FINRA RULES11620 AND 11630

Computation of interest (FINRA Rule 11620) - when a settlement is for interest paying securities, interest is to be added to the price. Interest is calculated on a 360-day year.

Due-bills and due-bill checks (FINRA Rule 11630) - a due-bill an instrument that is evidence of a transfer of a security and obligates the seller to deliver to the purchaser. A due-bill is not transferable or assignable. A due-bill check is a due-bill that is a check payable on the date of a cash dividend or interest payable. Prior to that date, a due-bill check is considered a due-bill. If a security is sold before it trades "ex-dividend" and the delivery is too late to make it on the record date, the delivery is to be accompanied with a due-bill for the additional distribution to be made. In this case, the contract is to be prorated based on this amount.

FINRA RULE 11640

If a buyer receives delivery of stock in time before the end of the closing of books on the record date, the buyer has no claim upon the seller for any dividends or rights, but the seller is to make its best effort to collect the same for the buyer. If a buyer requests the purchaser to collect dividends or rights pertaining to a stock that was not transferred in time, the seller can require the presentation of the certificate or a letter from the transfer agent proving the claim is true.

FINRA RULES 11650 AND 11700

Transfer fees (FINRA Rule 11650) - the party at whose instance a transfer is made is the party that shall pay any and all fees involved with being the transfer agent.

Reclamations and rejections (FINRA Rule 11700)

1. Reclamation definition - a claim for the right to return a security that has already been accepted.
2. Uniform Reclamation Form - must be included with a reclamation or return. If not, a sell-out is permitted.
3. Time for delivery of reclamation and manner of settlement - a security that has an irregularity can be returned during hours established by rule or practice in the community. When a security is being returned, the original party who delivered it is to give to the returning party immediately either the security in proper form or the cash amount of the contract.

FINRA RULE 11720

Irregular Delivery - Transfer Refused - Lost or Stolen Securities (FINRA Rule 11720)

1. Irregular delivery - a reclamation because of an irregularity in the delivery of a security is to take place within 30 months of the settlement date of the contract.
2. Transfer refused - a reclamation because the transfer agent has refused the transfer is to take place within 30 months of the settlement date of the contract.
3. Lost or stolen securities - a reclamation because of a lost or stolen security shall be within 30 months after the settlement date of the contract.

FINRA RULE 11740

If pursuant to a securities contract, a party in a transaction finds itself unsecured due to a change in the market price of an asset, that party can demand the contra-party to make a deposit equal to the difference between the market price and the contract price. If the market price changes again as to allow for a refund of the deposit, such refunds are to be made on demand. If these rules are not followed by a party, the other party is entitled to close the contract by making an offsetting purchase or sale contract.

FINRA RULE 11810

If a securities contract is not being completed by the seller, the buyer can close the contract after the third business day, except for in certain instances when the contract is subject to buy-in requirements of the securities exchange, when the contract is exempt by other provisions of the Exchange Act, and when the securities are issued by an investment company or direct participation program. In each instance that a buyer is to use this Rule, a notice of buy-in meeting specific requirements is to be delivered to the seller. This notice is to contain information including date the contract will be closed out, the quantity and value of the securities, the settlement date of the contract, and other material information.

FINRA RULE 11820

Selling-out (FINRA Rule 11820) - if a buyer does not accept the delivery of a contract and there is no properly executed Uniform Reclamation Form, the seller may sell-out the securities in the best available market. If performing a sell-out, the seller is to promptly notify the broker-dealer for whose account the securities were sold of the quantity sold and price received.

FINRA RULE 11840

Rights and warrants (FINRA Rule 11840)

1. Rights - are the privilege of holders of record to subscribe for additional securities. Transactions in rights are to be traded one right for one stock, and in blocks of 100.
2. Warrants - are instruments that can be issued either accompanying or separately from a stock, and represent the privilege to purchase shares at a specified price. Warrants are to be traded in blocks of 100, and each warrant is to specify what exactly it entitles the holder to purchase and at what price.

FINRA RULE 11860

COD orders (FINRA Rule 11860) - a member cannot enter into an agreement with a customer where the payment for securities purchased or delivery of securities sold is to be made by an agent of the customer unless all of the following procedures are followed:

1. agent information is to be obtained: name, address, and time and account number of customer on file.
2. each order from customer is notated as a payment on deliver (POD) or collect on deliver (COD) transaction.
3. the member is to deliver to the customer a confirmation of execution of order within one business day.
4. the member is to have an agreement with the customer that states the customer will give to the agent instructions regarding receipt or delivery of securities promptly after the customer receives each confirmation.
5. a clearing agency is to be used for book entry settlement.

FINRA RULE 11890

Authority to review transactions - the authority to review clearly erroneous transactions rests with FINRA's Market Regulation Department or Transparency Services Department for over-the-counter exchange listed securities that meet the thresholds requirements set forth.

Procedures for reviewing transaction - a FINRA officer can make a transaction null and void for the purposes of this rule if it is clearly erroneous or the action is necessary to ensure a fair and orderly market or for the protection of public interest. After a transaction is null and void, the parties involved in the transaction are notified. The aggrieved party can appeal the action.

System disruptions or malfunctions - the appropriate FINRA officer can take into account factors additional to those outlined in the thresholds to determine if a transaction is clearly erroneous, including any system disruptions or malfunctions.

FINRA RULE 11900

Clearance of corporate debt securities (FINRA Rule 11900) - member registered clearing agencies are to use the facilities of registered clearing agencies to clear over-the-counter corporate debt security transactions between members.

FINRA RULES 2140 AND 11870

Interfering with the transfer of customer accounts in the context of employment disputes (FINRA Rule 2140) - members are not to interfere with a customer's request to transfer his account because of a change in employment of the customer's registered representative.

Customer account transfer contracts (FINRA Rule 11870) - if a customer wants to transfer an account from one member to another, the members are obligated to coordinate and expedite the transfer. When a member receives a transfer instruction form (TIF) from a customer, the members is to send instructions to the carrying member. The carrying member has 1 day to validate the transfer or take exception to the transfer. Exceptions must be promptly resolved.

FINRA RULE 4320

Short sale delivery requirements (FINRA Rule 4320) - if a participant in a registered clearing agency has failed to deliver a security to fulfill a short sale for 13 consecutive days, he is to close out the position and purchase a security of like kind and quality. Until the participant closes out this position and purchases a security of like kind and quality, he is not to accept any additional short sale orders for the security. If the participant in a registered clearing agency reasonably allocates a portion of the failure to deliver to a broker-dealer for whom he clears transactions, then the rule is applied to the broker-dealer, not the participant. The participant is not exempted as stated if he has entered into an agreement to purchase securities for a person that he knows will not deliver during settlement.

OTC TRADE COMPARISON AND REGULAR WAY AND WHEN ISSUED CONTRACT SHEETS

OTC trade comparison - a clearing agency will accept and match one-sided transactions for over-the-counter securities. Once matched with a counter-side, the two parties are notified and the transaction is sent to the Continuous Net Settlement system for settling.

Regular way and when issued contract sheets - under a regular way contract sheet, transactions are settled on the 3rd business day after execution. This is the time when securities and funds actually exchange hands. Under a when issued contract, the physical security certificate actually does not exist yet, so the security will exchange hands when it is issued. When issued transactions usually happen in the primary market.

OTC SECURITIES, PINK SHEETS, THIRD MARKET, FOURTH MARKET AND OTC BULLETIN BOARD

Over-the-counter (OTC) Securities - securities that are traded via means other than formal exchanges.

Pink sheets - a daily compilation of OTC bid and ask prices.

Third market - the trading in exchange listed securities in OTC market.

Fourth market - the private transactions between institutional investors without the use of brokers/dealers. In this way, large investors such as mutual funds can avoid paying the commission fees of brokers/dealers.

OTC bulletin board - a listing of OTC security quotes. It allows participants to enter, update, and retrieve quotation information on non-NASDAQ OTC stocks on real-time basis. It displays firm quotes and un-priced indications of interest.

FINRA TRACE RULES
FINRA RULE 6710

TRACE-eligible security — a U.S. dollar denominated debt security of a private foreign entity pursuant to Securities Act Rule 144A.

Trade Reporting and Compliance Engine (TRACE) — FINRA's automated system that aids reporting of TRACE-eligible securities.

Reportable TRACE transactions — a transaction of a TRACE-eligible security that it not reported as in Rule 6730(e) and is a sale from an issuer to an underwriter as part of an offering.

Time of execution — the time at which all parties of a transaction agree to the terms.

TRACE participant — any FINRA member who reports to TRACE.

Introducing broker — FINRA member identified as a party to a transaction but who does not execute the transaction.

Investment grade — a TRACE-eligible security among the highest ratings of a nationally recognized rating organization.

Split-rated — a TRACE-eligible security that is rated by multiple nationally recognized rating organizations and is not in the same ratings category in each.

Agency — a U.S. executive agency that is authorized to issue debt or to guarantee the payment of the debt of another organization.

Money market instrument — a debt security that has a maturity of one year or less.

List or fixed offering price transaction — an initial offering purchased at the listed price.

Takedown transaction — an initial offering purchased below the listed price.

TRACE system hours — 8:00 AM Eastern Time to 6:29:59 PM Eastern Time.

Agency pass-through, mortgage-backed security — a mortgage backed security issued by an agency for which to principal and interest will pass-through to a pool of investors.

Specified pool transaction — a transaction of an agency pass-through mortgage-backed security.

Stipulation transaction — an agency pass-through mortgage-backed security transaction in which the investors stipulate the price and conditions.

Dollar role — a simultaneous sale and purchase of an agency pass-through mortgage-backed security.

FINRA Rule 6720

When to report - each member in a TRACE transaction is to report it within 15 minutes after the time of execution according to reporting requirements specific to the type of transaction.

Who reports the transaction - if two members are involved, both members are to report. If 1 member and a non-member, then the member is to report.

Information to be reported - information to be reported includes, CUSIP number, size, price, whether it is a buy or sell, date of execution, contra-party identifier, capacity, time of execution, commission, and date of settlement.

FINRA Rules 6740 and 6760

Termination of TRACE service (Rule 6740) - FINRA can terminate TRACE service to any member who does not abide by any of the rules.

Dissemination of transaction information (Rule 6750) - FINRA will disseminate reported transaction information immediately, with some exception.

Obligation to provide notice (Rule 6760) - it is the managing underwriter or group of underwriters obligation to obtain the CUSIP and provide notice to FINRA before the first transaction of an offering.

FINRA Rule 7110

Browse — TRACS function that allows for query and review of trades in the system.

Clearing broker-dealer — member firm recognized by TRACS as the principal for clearing/settling a trade.

Correspondent executing broker-dealer — member firm recognized by TRACS as having a correspondent relationship with a clearing firm.

Introducing broker-dealer — a FINRA member firm recognized by TRACS as a party to the transaction, but not the executor of the transaction.

Trade Reporting and Comparison Service (TRACS) — FINRA's automated system that is part of the Alternative Display Facility that reports and compares trade information.

TRACS ECN — FINRA member that is a registered ADF ECN that elects to display orders in the ADF.

TRACS market maker — a FINRA member that is a registered reporting ADF market maker.

TRACS order entry firm — a FINRA member that executes orders but is not a market maker.

FINRA RULES 7120, 7130, AND 7170

TRACS participation (Rule 7120) - participation in the TRACS trade comparison feature by participants in the alternative display facility is mandatory, and is contingent on specific obligations applicable to each participant type.

Trade report input (Rule 7130) - all transactions are required to be reported on by FINRA Rule 6280. TRACS trade comparison participants are to submit reports within 10 seconds after execution.

Termination of TRACS service (Rule 7170) - FINRA may terminate TRACS service if a participant fails to abide by any of the FINRA rules.

FINRA RULE 7220A

Trade reporting participation requirements - participation is mandatory for clearing agency members.

Participant obligations

1. Access - participants can access the service via computer or otherwise during the hours of operation.
2. System participant obligations - in order to beginning participation, a participant is to initially contact the System Operation Center for verification. A self-clearing firm must accept and clear all trades the system attributes to that firm. Introducing brokers or correspondent executing brokers are to identify their clearing broker and if said clearing broker is to be changed. If a participant fails to have a clearing arrangement, it will be removed from the system.
3. Clearing broker obligations - each clearing broker is to accept and clear all transactions effected by itself or its corresponding executing brokers.

FINRA RULE 7230A

When trade reports are submitted - participants are to transmit trade reports within 10 seconds after execution.

Who inputs trade reports - participants are to either input trade reports or, using the browse feature, accept or decline trades.

Trade information to be input - information to be input includes security identification symbol of the eligible security (SECID), number of shares, price, time of execution, indication that party is either on reporting member side or non-reporting member side, indication that transaction is a buy or sell, the reporting side clearing broker, reporting side executing broker, contra side executing broker, contra side introducing broker, and contra side clearing broker.

FINRA RULES 7240A AND 7270A

Trade report processing (FINRA Rule 7240A) - locked-in trades are to be determined in the system through one of the following methods:

1. Trade by trade match - both parties input transaction data and the system matches them together.
2. Trade acceptance - the reporting party inputs the information for his side of the trade, and the accepting party reviews and accepts or declines.
3. Aggregate volume match - at the end of the day, the system will add the volumes of uncompared trades reports and match based on that information.
4. T+N trade processing - trade reports are carried over to the next business day if not matched until 21 days later (T+21). After day 21 (T+22), they will be purged from the system.

Violation of reporting rules (FINRA Rule 7270A) - failure to comply with any of the rules will place participant in violation of Rule 2010.

FINRA RULE 7410

Bunched order — two or more orders added together before execution.

Customer — person other than a broker or dealer.

Electronic communication network (ECN) — any electronic system that disseminates orders entered by a market maker and allows orders to be executed.

Electronic order — order captured via an electronic order-routing system.

Manual order — order captured other than an electronic order-routing system.

Order audit trail system — FINRA's automated system that captures order information in National Market System (NMS) stocks and OTC equity securities for integrated trade and quote information providing accurate time and sequence of orders and transactions.

FINRA RULES 7420, 7430, 7440, AND 7450

Applicability (Rule 7420) - the requirements in FINRA Rule 7400 apply to all member brokers and dealers.

Synchronization of member business clocks (Rule 7430) - members are to synchronize, and maintain synchronized, their clocks used for time stamping.

Recording of order information includes (Rule 7440): A member is to immediately record order information. Information is to include an order identifier; FINRA assigned identification symbol of the security; market participant symbol; the department or terminal identification number; identification of agent; number of shares; whether it is a buy or sell order; whether it is a short sale or short sale exempt; whether it is a market order, limit order, stop order, or stop limit order; any limit or stop price; date of expiration; time limit; and date and time order received.

Order data transmission requirements (Rule 7450) - orders are to be transmitted electronically whenever an order is originated, transmitted, or received. A reporting member may enter into an agreement with a reporting agent.

NASDAQ RULE 4751

NASDAQ Market Center (or "system") — the automated system for order execution and trade reporting owned and operated by The NASDAQ Stock Market LLC. It comprised of an order execution service, a trade reporting service, and data feeds.

System securities — all securities listed on NASDAQ as well as all securities subject to the Consolidated Tape Association Plan and Consolidated Quotation Plan.

NASADQ ECNs — NASDAQ member participants that meet requirements found in Rule 4623.

NASDAQ market makers — NASDAQ member participants that are registered NASDAQ market makers.

Order entry firms — NASDAQ member participants registered as order entry firms and enter orders of NASDAQ securities into the system.

Quote — a single bid or offer quotation designated for display.

Automatic quote refresh — a default price increment away from the executed price and size. The quote is refreshed to it if the participant uses this functionality.

Reserve size — the system functionality that allows participants to display only part of a full order, and the rest to be held in reserve, undisplayed. The entire amount is executable against incoming orders. When the displayed portion drops below a certain amount, the system automatically replenishes it from the reserve portion.

Order — a single order or multiples orders at the same price.

Attributable orders — are designed for display with price and size next to the participants MPID.

Non-attributable orders — are entered by a participant for display anonymously.

Non-displayed orders — a limit order that is not displayed in the system, but is still available for potential execution by incoming orders.

Order type - describes the unique process for specific orders.

Discretionary orders - are displayed in the system and give a range within which the order can be executed.

Reserve orders - only part of a full order is displayed. The rest is held in reserve, undisplayed. The entire amount is executable against incoming orders. When the displayed portion drops below a certain amount, the system automatically replenishes it from the reserve portion.

Limit order - an order to buy or sell at a specific price or better.

Pegged order - an order with a price that is adjusted by the system after entry to match either an inside quote price or the midpoint of the national best offer.

Minimum quantity order - a minimum quantity must be obtained, or the order gets cancelled.

Intermarket sweep order (ISO) - an order that "sweeps" multiple market centers and buys shares of a security at multiple price levels.

Price to comply order - if the order would lock or cross the quote of an external market, the order is adjusted to match the current best price and then is displayed at one price increment better.

Price to comply post order - if the order would lock or cross the quote of a protected quote in an external market, the order is adjusted to match that price and then is displayed at one price increment worse.

Directed order - an order that is directed to an exchange outside of the NASDAQ by the entering party.

Post-only orders - if the order would lock an order on the system, the order is adjusted to match that price and then is displayed at one price increment worse.

Order size — the number of shares in an order up to 999,999. Includes normal unit of trading, mixed lot, and odd lot.

Normal unit of trading — round lot size for a security.

Mixed lot — an order for more than one normal trading unit, but not a full multiple.

Odd-lot — an order for less than one normal trading unit of a security.

System book feed — a data feed for NASDAQ eligible securities.

Time in force - the period of time the system will hold an order for potential execution.

System hours immediate or cancel (SIOC) - if the order is not marketable, it will be immediately canceled and returned.

System hours day (SDAY) - order will stay executable from 7 AM to 8 PM, Eastern Time on the day it was entered.

System hours good-til-canceled (SGTC) - order will stay executable for one year or until it is canceled by the entering party.

System hours expire time (SHEX) - order will stay executable until a time specified by the entering party, at which time they will be canceled.

Market hours IOC (MIOC) — if the order becomes unmarketable, the order or unexecuted portion will be cancelled and returned. If entered prior to 9:30 AM, the marketability of the order will be determined at 9:30 AM the day the order was placed.

Market hours day (MDAY) — order will be canceled and returned if not executed by 4 PM on the day of the order.

Market hours GTC (MGTC) — order will be good for 1 year after entry, available for execution between 9:30 AM and 4 PM Eastern Time.

Good-til-market close (GTMC) — order will be good until the market closes.

NASDAQ Rules 4755 and 4756

Order entry parameters (Rule 4755) - a system order is an order that is entered into the system for display and/or execution against contra-side orders in the system and contains the following parameters: limit price, whether it is a buy, short sale, or long sale, specify a time in force, and specify the order type.

Entry and display of quotes and orders (Rule 4756)

1. Entry - orders can be entered at single and multiple price levels. The system time-stamps each order and uses this for ranking the order for processing. Orders can be entered from 7 AM to 8 PM Eastern Time.
2. Display of quotes and orders
3. System book feed - quotes and orders in the system that are available for execution will be displayed via the system book feed.
4. Best priced order display - for each security, the total of all quotes and orders at the best price are sent to the network processor to be displayed.

NASDAQ Rule 4757 and 4761

Book processing - orders are executed according to the following:

1. Execution algorithm - the system executes equally or better priced orders in price/time priority in this order: displayed orders, non-displayed orders, and the discretionary portions of discretionary orders.
2. Decrementation - on execution, an order is reduced by the amount equal to that execution.
3. Price improvement - any price increase resulting from a trade goes to the taker of liquidity.

Adjustment of open quotes and/or orders (NASDAQ Rule 4761)

1. NASDAQ will automatically adjust the price or size of orders in response to issuer corporate actions related to dividends in the following manner:
2. Quotes - all bid and offer quotes are purged from the system.
3. Sell orders - are not adjusted, unless the entering party so desires and makes the modification.
4. Buy orders - are automatically adjusted by the system subject to certain conditions and criteria.

NASDAQ Rule 4758

DOT - after checking NASDAQ, orders are routed to other exchanges before arriving to the destination exchange. Any unexecuted portion at this point will be sent to the NYSE.

Reactive electronic only (STGY) - after checking NASDAQ, orders are routed to other exchanges. If orders remain unexecuted after routing, the system posts them on the book, where they wait until the price is crossed or locked, at which point the order will be sent to that market for execution.

Electronic only scan (SCAN) - after checking NASDAQ, orders are routed to other exchanges. If orders remain unexecuted after routing, the system posts them on the book. If the price is crossed or locked in another market, the orders will not be sent to the locking or crossing market.

NASDAQ Rules 4611, 4612, and 4619

NASDAQ Market Center participant registration (Rule 4611) - participation in NASDAQ requires current registration. Registration assumes compliance with numerous requirements including execution of applicable NASDAQ agreements, maintaining membership in a clearing agency, compliance with all rules, maintaining of physical security of equipment located at NASDAQ, accepting and settling any trade affected by registrant, and inputting accurate information.

Registration as a NASDAQ market maker (Rule 4612) - quotes can only entered by a registered NASDAQ market maker. To be registered, a request is to be submitted via the approved electronic NASDAQ interface or by contacting NASDAQ Market Operations. Registration will be terminated if market maker fails to enter quotes within five days after registration in a security becomes effective.

Withdrawal of quotations and passive market making (Rule 4619) - a market maker that wishes to withdraw their quotations of a security or have the listed as a passive market maker is to contact NASDAQ MarketWatch to obtain an excused withdrawal status prior to actually withdrawing its quotes. Excused withdrawal status is approved based on certain conditions.

SECURITIES EXCHANGE ACT OF 1934 TERMS

Dealer — any person engaging in business to buy and sell securities for his client's account, not including individuals trading on their own account or as a fiduciary responsibility to another (Section 3(a)(5)).

Clearing agency — any person acting as an intermediary making payments or deliveries for securities transactions, or who provides comparison data, in order to reduce the number of settlements of transactions or to allocate settlement responsibilities (Section 3(a)(23)(A)).

Market maker — a dealer who is continuously willing to buy and sell a specific security for his own account (Section 3(a)(38)).

Listed — given full trading privileges upon application of the issuer (Rule 3b-1).

Qualified OTC market maker — a dealer transacting in over-the-counter securities that is registered and meets certain financial requirements (Rule 3b-8).

Qualified third market maker — a registered market that meets certain financial requirements, transacting in a stock that is registered on a national exchange (Rule 3b-8).

Qualified block positioner — a registered dealer that meets certain financial requirements, engaging in purchasing long or selling short from or to a customer a block of stock with a value of at least $200,000 (Rule 3b-8).

SEC RULE 3A51-1

Definition of penny stock (SEC Rule 3a51-1) - Rule 3a51-1 defines penny stock by describing what a penny stock is not. The definition includes any equity security that:

1. is not a security continuously registered on a national securities exchange;
2. is not a registered security on a national securities exchange that meets certain criteria;
3. is not issued by an investment company registered by the Investment Company Act of 1940;
4. is not a put or call option from an Options Clearing Corporation;
5. does not have a price of $5 or more.

SEC RULE 15G-1

Exemptions for certain transactions (SEC Rule 15g-1) - the following transactions are exempt from Rules 15g-2, 15g-3, 15g-4, 15g-5, and 15g-6:

1. Transactions by a broker/dealer whose commissions from penny stock transactions do not exceed 5% of total commissions and who has not been a market maker in a penny stock.
2. Transactions with an institutional investor as the customer.
3. Transactions that meet the requirements in Regulation D.
4. Transactions with the issuer, director, or other person who owns more than 5% of the issuers stock as the customer.
5. Transactions that are not recommended by the broker/dealer.
6. Other transactions exempted by the SEC.

SEC RULES 15G-2 AND 15G-3

Risk disclosure document relating to the penny stock market (SEC Rule 15g-2) - a broker/dealer must have the customer sign a Schedule 15G document before transacting in penny stocks in the customer's account. The broker/dealer cannot transact in penny stocks on behalf of the customer within two days of sending such document, and must keep a copy of this document in records.

Broker or dealer disclosure of quotations and other information relating to the penny stock market (SEC Rule 15g-3) - a broker/dealer must disclose to the customer the inside bid/offer quotes and the number of shares applicable before transacting in penny stock on behalf of the customer.

SEC RULES 15G-4 AND 15G-5

Disclosure of compensation to brokers or dealers (SEC Rule 15g-4) - a broker/dealer must disclose to the customer the total compensation received in connection with transaction before transacting in penny stock on behalf of the customer.

Disclosure of compensation of associated persons in connection with penny stock transactions (SEC Rule 15g-5) - a broker/dealer must disclose to the customer the total compensation received by any associated person of the broker/dealer in connection with the transaction before transacting in penny stock on behalf of the customer.

SEC RULES 15G-6 AND 15G-9

Account statements for penny stock customers (SEC Rule 15g-6) - a broker/dealer must send a monthly account statement to customers within ten days following the end of the month during which they have transacted in penny stocks.

Sales practice requirements for certain low priced securities (SEC Rule 15g-9) - a broker/dealer must approve a customer's account for trading in penny stocks using specific criteria. The broker/dealer must receive an agreement from the customer to a specific transaction in penny stocks, and cannot make the transaction until after two days from sending such document to the customer.

ATS, SEC REGULATION ATS, AND ECNS

Alternative trading systems - are non-exchange trading systems that find counterparts for transactions.

SEC Regulation ATS - sets requirements that govern alternative trading systems.

Electronic Communications Networks (ECNs) - an electronic ATS that anonymously finds counterparts for transactions.

REGULATION M
RULES 100 AND 104

Stabilize or stabilizing (Rule 100) - to bid or purchase with the internet to peg, fix, or maintain the securities' price.

Stabilizing bids (Rule 104) - are only allowed for the purpose of stabilizing the price of the security. They are not allowed for the purposes of manipulating the market. Only one stabilizing bid can be entered at the same prince in the same market, and the price can be no more than the offering price. After the bid is entered, it can be increased to a maximum of equal to the highest independent bid, and can be decreased regardless of independent bids.

REGULATION NMS
RULE 600

Block size - an order of at least 10,000 shares or a quantity of stock valued at least at $200,000.

Electronic communications network - an electronic system that reports to third parties the orders entered, allowing them to be executed.

Exchange market maker - a member of a national exchange that is a registered specialist or market maker.

Exchange-traded security - an NMS security with trading privileges on a national securities exchange.

NMS security/stock - a security for which reports of transactions are available pursuant to an effective transaction reporting plan.

OTC market maker - a dealer willing to continuously buy and sell a certain NMS securities for its own account in amounts less than block size.

Quotation size - the number of shares specified by a broker or dealer willing to purchase or sell the security.

SEC RULES 602 AND 604

Obligations of responsible brokers and dealers in the dissemination of quotations in NMS securities - each responsible broker or dealer is to promptly communicate to the applicable national securities exchange its best bids, offers, and quotation sizes for any subject security.

Display customer limit orders for specialists and OTC market makers- members of national securities exchanges who are specialists or OTC market makers are to immediately publish a bid or offer that reflects:

1. the price and full size of each customer limit order that would improve the bid or offer of the specialist;
2. the full size of each customer limit order priced equal to the specialist's best bid or offer, equal to the national best bid, and that represents more than a de minimis change in the specialist's bid or offer.

SEC RULES 605, 606, AND 607

Disclosure of order execution information - every market center is to make available monthly a report on the covered orders in NMS stocks, and the report is to include specific information including the number of covered orders, and average spread (SEC Rule 605).

Disclosure of order routing information - every broker or dealer is to make available quarterly a report on its routing of non-directed orders in NMS securities. The report is to include information regarding the percentage of non-directed orders and venues that non-directed orders were sent to. If a customer requests it, the broker/dealer must disclose the venue that the customer's order were sent to (SEC Rule 606).

Customer account statements - a broker or dealer acting as an agent must inform their customers upon opening an account and yearly thereafter of the following: the policies regarding receipt of payment for order flow, and the policies for determining where to route customer orders that are the subject of payment (SEC Rule 607).

RULES 611 AND 612

Order protection rule (trade-throughs) - trading centers must have policies and procedures to prevent trade-throughs, and must regularly review the policies to ascertain the effectiveness (Rule 611).

Minimum pricing increments - an offer or order cannot be accepted for less than $0.01 if the security is priced at $1.00 per share or more. If the security is priced at less than $1.00 per share, the offer or order cannot be for less than $0.0001 (Rule 612).

REGULATION SHO AND REGULATION M
REGULATIONS SHO

1. Definition of short sale (Rule 200) - a sale of a security that the seller does not own, or a sale in which the delivered security was borrowed by the seller.
2. Borrowing and delivery requirements (Rule 203) - in order to perform short sales on behalf of his customers, a broker-dealer must have:
3. borrowed the security; or
4. reason to believe the security can be borrowed and is deliverable on the due date, and has documented its compliance to the rule.
5. Any list of available securities must be no more than 24 hours old.

REGULATION M

A. Short selling in connection with a public offering (Rule 105) - it is prohibited for anyone to sell short a security a part of a public offering and buy the security from an underwriter or broker-dealer participating in the offering during a restricted period defined as beginning five days before the pricing of the security and ending at the pricing, or between the initial filing of the registration statement and the pricing.

REGULATION M RULE 103

As an exception to Rule 101 that prevents distribution participants to bid for or purchase a covered security during the restricted period, Rule 103 states that passive market makers are allowed to engage in market making transactions in covered NASDAQ securities as long as certain conditions are met.

NYSE RULE 410A AND 410B

Automated submission of trading data (NYSE Rule 410A) - a member is to transmit trade data in an automated format that is to include clearing house number, identifying symbol, date of execution, number of shares, transaction price, account number, and market center.

Reports of listed securities transactions effected off the Exchange (NYSE Rule 410B) - a member that has transacted a trade off of the Exchange is to report it to the exchange by the close of the next business day. The reports must contain information including time and date of transaction; stock symbol; number of shares; price; marketplace where transaction was executed; indication of whether it was buy, sell, or cross; whether transaction was executed as principal or agent; and contra side broker-dealer.

TWO-SIDED QUOTE OBLIGATION, PRICING OBLIGATIONS FOR REGISTERED REPORTING ADF MARKET MAKERS, AND NATIONAL BEST BID AND OFFER

Two-sided quote obligation - for every security that an ADF market maker is registered, the market maker must be willing to buy and sell the security on a continuous basis and maintain a two-sided trading interest.

Pricing obligations for registered reporting ADF market makers - for bids and offers, the price is not to be more than a certain percentage away from the national best bid at the time.

National best bid and offer - is determined by FINRA.

NYSE RULE 123D

NYSE Rule 123D - Designated market makers (DMMs) are to ensure that registered securities open as close to the opening bell as possible. In the event that this is not possible, there are specific rules to follow. The NYSE has established processes for certain trading halts including equipment changeover, investment company units or index-linked securities, and dissemination of net asset value.

1. Equipment changeover - applicable when trading in a certain security is inhibited due to systems or equipment concerns.
2. Investment company units or index-linked securities - applicable in regards to investment company units or index-linked securities to allow for "closing the room."
3. Dissemination of net asset value - applicable when the NYSE sees that net asset value information is not being disseminated to all market participants at the same time.

MINIMUM LISTING STANDARDS FOR AUCTION EXCHANGE MARKETS AND NYSE-LISTED COMPANY MANUAL

Minimum listing standards - in order to be originally listed on a stock exchange, there are minimum financial and non-financial standards that a company must meet. The criteria include standards in market value, stock price, and number of publicly traded shares.

NYSE-listed company manual - the comprehensive rule-book for companies listed on the NYSE.

TRADING POST AND NYSE RULES 54, 104A, 116, AND 115A

Trading post - a location on the trading floor of the NYSE where the offers of buyers and sellers are matched for execution.

Floor brokers - only members are able to make bids or offers or consummate any transaction on the trading floor.

Role of designated market makers:

1. Maintain the limit order book.
2. General (Rule 104A) - maintain a record of all sales and purchases, including options and foreign securities.
3. "Stop" constitutes guarantee (Rule 116) - if a DMM makes a stop agreement at a specific price, it means that the member guarantees execution at that price.
4. Orders at opening or unusual situations (Rule 115A) - DMMs arrange buy and sell orders at the opening of daily trading to orchestrate a balanced price.

AUTOMATED TRADING SYSTEM

An automated trading system automatically submits trades. The NYSE has DOT, PACE, AUTO, AMOS, and SCOREX.

NYSE RULE 127

If a member received an order for sale or purchase of a block of securities at a price that may not be absorbed by the market, the member is to talk to DMMs on the floor to gauge their interest in participating.

NYSE RULES 61, 76, AND 77

Recognized quotations rules - bids and offers for more than one trading unit are executable for any lesser number of trading units. A transaction greater than one trading unit but not a multiple thereof will be published to the consolidated tape and may qualify for last trade. A transaction for less than one trading unit is not reported to the consolidated tape and does not qualify for last trade.

Crossing orders - if a member has an order to buy and an order to sell in the same security, the member must price it a margin above its own bid, and such crossing transactions must be announced.

Prohibited dealings and activities - it is prohibited to buy/sell securities on stop above or below market, to buy/sell securities at the close, to buy/sell dividends, to bet upon the course of the market, or to buy/sell privileges to receive or deliver securities.

Supervision of Investment Banking and Research

FINRA Rules 2262 and 2269

Rule 2262 states that if common control exists between a member firm and the issuer of a security, the firm must disclose the relationship in writing to any customer wanting to buy or sell said security. For example, if Firm A is selling an equity security in Company B to a customer and Firm A and Company B have a common majority owner, this relationship has to be disclosed to the customer.

Rule 2269 states that if a firm is participating in or has a financial interest in any security either in primary or secondary distribution, this has to be disclosed in writing to the customer. For example, if a firm will receive a financial gain from a specific equity security, this must be disclosed to the customer before selling this same equity to a customer.

FINRA Rule 5110

Underwriting compensation and arrangements - all underwriting terms and agreements have to be fair and reasonable. All compensation in relation to underwriting a security has to be fair and reasonable.

Items included in compensation - all items of value received or that will be received by an underwriter in connection with a distribution starting from 180 days before the filing date are considered to be compensation and have to be disclosed in the prospectus.

Valuation of non-cash compensation - a security cannot be received by an underwriter as compensation in connection with a public offering unless the security is identical to the security issued to the public or the security can be accurately valued. Calculated compensation value is usually in some way based on, or derived from, the market price or public offering price.

Non-cash compensation - is restricted, and includes small gifts, occasional meals, and entertainment events.

Net offering proceeds — all offering proceeds minus expenses of issuance and distribution.

Offering proceeds — total public offering price of securities offered to public.

Participating members — any FINRA member involved in the offering and associates.

Participating in public offering — involvement in any preparation, distribution, solicitation, or advisory activities of a public offering.

Underwriter and related persons — underwriter and counsel, consultants, advisors, finders, members, or any relative of each.

Listed securities — any securities meeting the listing standards of Securities Act Rule 146, any markets registered under the Exchange Act, and any markets offshore meeting requirements of Rule 902(b) in Regulation S.

103

Issuer — the issuer, affiliates, or security holders selling securities to the public including the corporate officers of each.

Derivative instruments — any eligible OTC derivative instrument defined in the Exchange Act Rule 3b-13(a).

Fair price — a price reached by underwriters in good faith, at arm's length, on a commercially reasonable basis, and according to appropriate pricing models.

Company — any legal organization or group of persons, incorporated or otherwise.

Effective date — first date the security is legal for distribution to public.

Immediate family — any relative in the same household with a member.

Person — a natural person or legally formed entity.

Filing requirements - in timely fashion as specified, FINRA requires various information to be submitted including: copies of registration statement, underwriting agreement, pre and post-effective amendment to registration, and final registration statement.

Unreasonable terms and arrangements - when an offering has been deemed to have terms and arrangements that are unreasonable or unfair, all transactions are to cease.

Lock-up restrictions on securities - for 180 days after an offering goes public, certain individuals such as majority stakeholders and company insiders are prohibited from trading their securities.

FINRA RULE 5121

Beneficial ownership — a right to economic benefits of a security.

Bona fide public market — the market for a security of certain issuers when the issuer has met registration requirements and has an average daily trading volume of $1 million.

Common equity — total number of common stock shares.

Conflict of interest — arises when a member participating in a public offering issues the securities or is an affiliate with the issuer, or certain cases when the member has a beneficial interest in the security.

Control — a person has control over another in certain instances when he has 10% or more ownership in the controlled person.

Entity — any legally formed entity, excluding certain investment companies, separate accounts, REITs, and direct participation programs.

Investment grade rated — is in the highest four rating categories of a nationally recognized rating organization.

Preferred equity — the total amount of preferred stock owned in a company.

Prominent disclosure — a disclosure of conflict of interest pursuant to the Rule.

Public Offering — any primary or secondary offering of securities made under a registration statement.

Qualified independent underwriter — certain underwriters who do not have a conflict of interest.

Subordinated debt — corporate debt that has a lower priority in being paid relating to other debt.

Public offerings of securities with conflicts of interest (FINRA Rule 5121) - no member with a conflict of interest can participate in certain public offerings unless the conflict is properly disclosed, a qualified independent underwriter has prepared it, the security is investment grade, and there is a bona fide public market.

Offerings resulting in affiliation or public ownership of member - when comprising more than 5% of the offering, it creates a conflict of interest.

Escrow of proceeds - any member offering securities under the Rule must place all proceeds in an escrow account where they must stay until the member is able to prove that they meet the net capital requirement, which requires the member to have enough funds to pay off certain obligations such as non-subordinated debt.

Discretionary accounts - no member with a conflict of interest may sell to a discretionary account.

FINRA RULES 5122, 5141, AND 11880

Placements of securities issued by members (FINRA Rule 5122) - no member can offer a private placement without properly disclosing the intended use of the proceeds and the offering expenses. The offering must file a private placement memorandum with the Corporate Financing Department.

Sale of securities in a fixed price offering (FINRA Rule 5141) - in a fixed price offering, no member can offer the securities at a price below the price stated in the offering.

Settlement of syndicate accounts (FINRA Rule 11880, previously NASD Rule 11880) - the syndicate manager is to settle the syndicate accounts, which were created by the syndicate members to purchase the offering from the issuer, no later than 90 days past the syndicate settlement date. The settlement date is the date the securities were delivered to the syndicate members. The manager is also to deliver expense statements to the members.

FINRA RULE 5130

General prohibitions - a member or associated person may not sell a new issue to a restricted person, or buy a new issue in an account in from which he himself benefits. A member cannot hold new issues acquired as an underwriter or selling group member. Rule 5130 provides exceptions including transactions between members that are incidental, transactions by a broker with non-restricted persons, and certain instances of investment partnerships.

Preconditions for sale - in order for an account to purchase a new issue, it must represent that it is eligible to purchase according to this rule through either its authorized representative, or bank, broker, or other conduit.

General exemptions - the prohibitions do not apply to certain investment companies, common trusts funds, insurance companies, accounts with restricted persons having less than 10% of the interest, publicly traded entities, foreign investment companies, and retirement plans.

Issuer-directed securities - the prohibitions of Rule 5130 do not apply in certain situations (1) when the issuer directs the securities to otherwise restricted persons, (2) when directed by issuer and no broker-dealer is involved, (3) when securities are a part of an issuer sponsored program, and (4) when part of a conversion offering.

Stand-by purchasers - prohibitions do not apply in certain situations where the purchase is pursuant to a stand-by agreement.

Undersubscribed offerings - the rule does not prohibit underwriters from placing a portion of the offering in its investment account when the portion could not be sold to public.

Anti-dilution provisions - the prohibitions do not apply in certain situations when (1) a restricted person has been an equity owner from more than one year, (2) the purchase does not increase the percentage ownership in issuer above a level equal to the level three months prior, (3) no special terms are involved, and (4) the security will not be transferred for three months.

FINRA RULE 5160

Each underwriter member of a syndicate can either sell the securities, or enlist the aid of agents to sell the securities. These agents along with the underwriter that enlisted them are considered a selling group. The agents receive compensation from the underwriter member that enlisted them in the form of a concession. The group is managed by the managing underwriter.

Selling agreement - each selling group is governed by a selling group agreement. FINRA Rule 5160 states that selling group agreements have to include the price at which the securities are sold to the public and what concessions if any are allowed to be given.

Liability - there are two different agreements among underwriters that divide the liability of any unsold portion of the issue differently:

1. Undivided (Eastern) - each syndicate member is responsible for all of the unsold securities in an issue, according to their percentage of participation.
2. Divided (Western) - each syndicate member is responsible for the unsold securities of only their portion of the issue.

FINRA RULE 5190

FINRA Rule 5190 outlines the required notifications for new public offerings. It provides requirements for securities subject to a restricted period under SEC Regulation M as well as actively traded securities:

1. Securities subject to a restricted period - a written notice must be submitted relaying to FINRA information regarding whether a one-day or five-day restricted period applies (according to Rule 101 of SEC Regulation M), the name and symbol of the security, the type of security, identification of participants and purchasers, the pricing, and the number of shares offered, among other things.
2. Actively traded securities - a written notice must be submitted relaying to FINRA information regarding the fact that no restrictive period applies, the name and symbol of the security, the type of security, identification of participants and purchasers, the pricing, and the number of shares offered, among other things.

FINRA Rule 5190 outlines the required notifications for penalty bids and syndicate covering transactions. When a member is imposing a penalty bid or is conducting a syndicate covering transaction, a written notice must be submitted relaying to FINRA information regarding the intent to carry out the activity and identification of the security and symbol, before imposing the bid or conducting the transaction. A confirmation is to be submitted to FINRA within one business day of the completion of the activity, including identification of the security and symbol, the total number of shares, and the date of the activity.

FINRA RULE 6130

Transactions related to initial public offerings (FINRA Rule 6130) - a member is not to execute a transaction outside of an exchange in an initial public offering security until the security has been opened for trading on a national securities exchange.

Obligation of lead underwriter - it is the obligation of the lead underwriter to notify NASDAQ the IPO has been released by the SEC.

NASDAQ RULES 4614 AND 4624

Stabilizing bid - means to stabilize as in SEC Rule 100.

Stabilizing bids (SEC Rule 4614):

1. Limitations on stabilizing bids - a stabilizing bid can only be entered if at least one other NASDAQ market maker is registered for the security, and the bid has to be available for all of the outstanding shares of the specific security.
2. Submission request - a market maker has to submit a request to NASDAQ in order to place a stabilizing bid.

Penalty bids and covering transactions (SEC Rule 4624) - a NASDAQ market maker has to submit written notice to FINRA prior to a penalty bid or syndicate covering transaction.

PLACEMENT AGENT, FINDER, AND SEC RULE 3A4-1

Placement agents - a placement agent is hired by a company to find and identify potential investors. Placement agents perform detailed due diligence and are usually registered brokers or dealers under FINRA regulation. They help with the fundraising preparation.

Finders - a finder is hired by a company to find and identify potential investors. However, they usually perform little to no due diligence. They are usually not registered or regulated by FINRA. They do not help with fundraising preparation, such as offering materials.

SEC Rule 3a4-1 states that certain persons associated with the issuer conducting limited securities sales is not considered to be a broker and therefore does not have to register as a broker according to Section 15 of the Securities Exchange Act.

SEC RULE 10B-9 AND SEC RULE 15C2-4

All or none offerings (SEC Rule 10b-9) - underwriters must sell all securities at the stated price and must pay the issuer, each within a given time frame.

Transmission or maintenance of payments received in connection with underwritings (SEC Rule 15c2-4) - underwriter must promptly pay the issuer any consideration due him after the sale of securities. If the issuer is to be paid at a later date as per the underwriting contract, the funds are to be placed into a trust or escrow account pursuant to conditions laid forth.

SECTION 12 OF THE SEA

All securities transacted on a securities exchange need to be registered (12a). Also, large issuers involved in interstate commerce are required to register securities with the SEC. Large issuers are issuers with more than $10,000,000 in assets and either more than 2,000 investors or more than 500 non-accredited investors (12g).

The SEC has the authority to revoke or suspend (up to 12 months) the registration of any security where the issuer has failed to comply with the Securities Exchange Act of 1934 (12j). The SEC also has the authority to suspend the trading of a security or of a national exchange market if needed for the protection of investors. The SEC can alter, supplement, suspend, or impose requirements during an emergency (12k).

FORMS AND SCHEDULES

Form 8-K - (Rule 13a-11/Rule 15d-11) - for current reports, every registrant has to file.

Form 10-K (Rule 13a-13/Rule 15d-13) - for annual reports, every registered issuer has to file.

Form 10-Q (Rule 13a-13/Rule 15d-13) - for quarterly reports, every registered issuer has to file.

Form 13D and 13G (Rule 13d-1) - 13D and 13G are beneficial ownership reports. 13D is to be filed within ten days after any person acquires more than 5% of a class of securities in a company. 13G is to be filed by a person within 45 days after the end of the calendar year in which the person filed a *short-form* 13D, and it reports the person's beneficial interest as of the last day of the calendar year.

Schedule 13E-3 (Rule 13e-3) - for going-private transactions, which are transaction where an issuer or affiliate buys back securities from stockholders. Schedule 13e-3 is required, as well as prompt amendments, a final amendment, and certain disclosures to the security holders.

Schedule 13F (Rule 13f-1) - required for any institutional investment manager whose accounts have at least $100 million in investments within 45 days of the end of the calendar year.

Form 14A (Rule 14a-6) - required for proxy statements, ten days before the proxy statements are sent to security holders.

Form 3 and Form 4 (Rule 16a-1) - beneficial ownership reports of directors, officers and principal stockholders with 10% or more of the security. Form 3 is filed when one of these individuals makes a first transaction after an IPO. Form 4 is used for subsequent transactions.

SEC RULE 13E-4 AND 14E-1

Filing requirements (SEC Rule 13e-4) - on the date of the issuer tender offer, the person making the offer must file with the SEC a Schedule TO, as well as all communication in relation starting from the first public announcement.

Unlawful tender offer practices (SEC Rule 14e-1)

1. A tender offer must be open for at least 20 days.
2. If the offer amount or purchase price is changed, the offer must stay open for ten more days.
3. Offered compensation must be paid promptly.
4. If an offer is to be extended passed the original date, it must be publicly announced.

SEC RULES 14E-2, 14E-3, 14E-4, AND 14E-5

Position of subject company (14e-2) - within ten days of a tender offer, the company must send to shareholders a notice as to whether or not they recommend accepting or have no opinion.

Non-public material tender offer information (14e-3) - a person having non-public material information in connection with a tender offer can be liable for insider trading.

Prohibited partial tender offer transactions (14e-4) - prohibits a person from tendering stocks that they do not own in a partial tender offer.

Purchases outside of a tender offer (14e-5) - the person making the tender offer is prohibited from acquiring the subject's securities through means outside of the tender offer.

RULES 15C1-5 AND 15C1-6

Disclosure of control - if a broker or dealer is under common control with a security that it deals, it must disclose this relationship to the customer before entering into a contract for said security with the customer (Rule 15c1-5).

Disclosure of interest in distributions - if a broker or dealer is a participant in or has any financial interest in a securities distribution and buys or sells this same security on the behalf of a paying customer, it must disclose this financial interest to the customer at or before the completion of the transaction (Rule 15c1-6).

SEC RULE 17A-2

The Rule applies to any person involved in purchasing securities for the purpose of stabilizing.

Definitions

1. Manager — the person organizing the selling efforts of the issuer and acting to stabilize the security.
2. Exempted security — a security considered exempt as per Section 3(a)(12) of the Securities Exchange Act.

Record keeping requirements - the manager is to promptly record and maintain certain information including: the name and class of the security, the price, date, and time of each stabilizing purchase, the names and addresses of the syndicate members, the respective commitment of each syndicate member, and the dates the penalty bid was in effect.

Manager notification requirements - any non-manager syndicate member who makes a stabilizing bid must notify the manager within three business days.

SEC RULE 144A

Only qualified institutional buyers are allowed to resell private placements. Qualified institutional buyers include certain insurance companies, investment companies and investment advisers, employee benefit plans, trusts, and business development companies. Qualified institutional buyers must own and invest a minimum of $100 million in securities.

Conditions to be met - the securities can only be sold to qualified institutional buyers; the seller must take steps to ensure the purchaser is aware the seller relies on the exemption; and securities cannot be of the same class as securities listed on a national exchange (with some exception).

SEC RULE 145

1. The Rule clarifies the situations in a reorganization (merger, consolidation, etc) in which an organization may need to register or be exempt from registration.
2. Transactions requiring registration:
   a. If a security is being reclassified, with the substitution of a security with another security.
   b. If existing securities will be converted from one company to another.

   c. If assets are to be transferred to an owner as compensation for shares.

3. Transactions that do not require registration:
   a. stock splits/reverse splits.
   b. change in par value.

Communications allowed - before a registration is filled, communications with the securities holders relating to the voting on issues regarding the reorganization are allowed.

Underwriters - if a shell company is involved in the voting on a reorganization, any person relating to the shell company that offers or sells securities of the issuer is an underwriter.

Resale provisions - certain persons are deemed to not be an underwriter if a certain amount of time has passed and certain requirements are met.

Form S-4 - an SEC filing that registers securities pursuant to Rule 145.

SEC RULE 147

Rule 147 provides standards for those relying on section 3(a)(11) exemptions. In order for these exemptions to be available, the issuer has to be a resident of and doing business in the same state that all offers and sales are made. There can be no non-resident purchasers. All offers and transactions that are part of the same issue must meet these requirements.

Transactions covered - all offers and transactions made by an issuer in compliance with the entire Rule.

Part of an issue - all securities that are part of the same issue must be sold in accordance with the Rule. Securities sold six months or more prior to, or six months or more after, an issue are not part of the same issue.

Nature of the issuer - the issuer has to be at the time of any offers or sales a resident of the state he is doing business in.

Offerees and purchasers: person resident - offers and transactions can only be made to and with residents of the same state in which the issuer is a resident.

Limitation of resales - for nine months after the last sale by the issuer, securities cannot be resold to any person not a resident of the same state.

Precautions against interstate offers and sales:

1. The issuer must, for any securities under the Rule:
   a. place a legend on the security document stating that the securities have not been registered.
   b. issue a stop transfer to its transfer agent or notate the same in the appropriate records if the issuer transfers his own securities.
   c. obtain written proof as to the residence of each purchaser.
2. The issuer must, with any offer or transaction, disclose the restrictions on resale to the buyer.

SECTION 4 OF THE SECURITIES ACT OF 1933

The following are types of transactions exempt from registration according to Section 4 of the Securities Act of 1933:

1. Transactions by anyone other than an issuer, underwriter, or dealer (Section 4(a)(1)).
2. Transactions that do not involve any public offering (Section 4(a)(2)).
3. Transactions by a dealer, except in certain instances within the first 40 days after the bona fide public offering or registration effective date, or pertaining to unsold allotments of securities (Section 4(a)(3)).
4. Transactions by a broker based on the order of a customer, but the solicitation of the order is not exempt (Section 4(a)(4)).
5. Certain transactions that are only offered to accredited investors (Section 4(a)(5)).
6. Certain transactions that are not more than a total of $1,000,000 dollars and that make no sales to an individual investor that are more than:
   a. the greater of $2,000 or 5% or the investors' annual income if the investor does not make more than $100,000 per year or
   b. 10% of the investors' annual income, with a maximum of $100,000, if the investor makes more than $100,000 per year (Section 4(a)(6)).

AMENDMENTS BEFORE AND AFTER REGISTRATION EFFECTIVE DATE, STOP ORDERS, AND SB-1 AND SB-2 FILINGS

Amendments to registration statement prior to effective date - are considered to be effective at the same time as the registration statement.

Amendments to registration statement after effective date - are effective on a date as determined by the SEC.

Stop orders - the SEC can issue a stop order, suspending the effectiveness of a registration, within 15 days of giving notice to do as such.

SB-1 filing requirements - Form SB-1 is used for registration of securities if the issuer has less than $25 million in revenue and the issue is for less than $10 million.

SB-2 filing requirements - From SB-2 is used for registration of securities if the issuer is a small business with less than $25 million in revenue and public float and the issue is sold for cash. SB-2 requires less information than SB-1.

SECTIONS 11, 12, AND 15 OF THE SECURITIES ACT

Registration statements (Section 11 of the Securities Act) - if there is any untrue statement or omission in a registration statement, the purchaser of the security can sue.

Prospectuses and communications (Section 12 of the Securities Act) - if there is any untrue statement or omission in a prospectus or communication, the purchaser of the security can sue. Pertaining to a law suit regarding this, only information given to the purchaser before the time of sale will be considered, not information conveyed after the purchase (SEC Rule 159). Any modification or amendment of a prospectus or communication is not an admission of an originally untrue statement or omission (SEC Rule 412).

Controlling persons (Section 15 of the Securities Act)- any personal controlling a person liable under Section 11 or 12 of the Securities Act - through stock ownership, agency, or otherwise - is also liable unless he had no knowledge basis regarding the untrue statement or omission.

SECTIONS 17, 23, 175, AND 3B-6

Fraudulent interstate transactions (Section 17 of the Securities Act) - it is illegal for anyone to engage in interstate activities that use a scheme to defraud, that obtain money with an untrue statement or omission, or conduct any business that would defraud or deceive a purchaser.

Unlawful representations (Section 23 of the Securities Act)- simply because a registration statement is in effect and there is no stop order on a specific security does not mean the SEC has assured the merits of or approved the security. Any effort to make a customer believe otherwise to make a sale is illegal.

Certain forward-looking statements (SEC Rule 175 and 3b-6) - certain statements such as forward-looking statements, projections, and plans are not fraudulent so long as they are reasonably believed to be true at the time they are made.

SEC RULE 405

Affiliate - a person who directly or indirectly controls or is under common control with the specified person.

Amount - for debt, it means the principal; for shares it means the number of shares; and it means the number of units if relating to any other security.

Associate - in reference to an organization, it is a person who is an officer, partner, or the beneficial owner of at least 10% or more of any class of securities. In reference to a trust or estate, it is anyone who is a trustee or has any interest in it. Relatives are also associates.

Automatic shelf registration statement - a shelf registration filed by a WKSI (well-known seasoned issuer).

Business combination related shell company - a company formed to combine multiple other businesses, or to change the corporate domicile of an existing company.

Dividend or interest investment plan — a plan that allows current security holders to reinvest dividends or interest.

Electronic filer — a person or entity that submits filings according to Rule 100 and 101.

Electronic filing — document submitted to the SEC in electronic format.

Employee — does not include director, trustee, or officer.

Employee benefit plan — a written purchase, saving, option, bonus, appreciation, profit sharing, thrift, incentive, pension, or similar plan available to employees.

Equity security — any stock, certificate of interest, transferable shares, limited partnership interest, joint venture interest, and certificate of interest. Any security entitling a person to interest in equity.

Executive officer — any president, vice president, or other policy making officer.

Fiscal year — either calendar year or other annual accounting period.

Foreign government — government of foreign country.

Foreign issuer — a foreign government, foreign person, or organization formed under the laws of a foreign government.

Foreign private issuer — certain foreign issuers other than foreign governments.

Free writing prospectus — a written communication that is an offer to transact a security meeting certain requirements.

Graphic communication — all forms of electronic media that are not being communicated in real-time (live).

Ineligible issuer — an issuer who has not met certain filing requirements put forth by the Securities Exchange Act of 1934 or violated other SEC rules and regulations.

Majority-owned subsidiary — a subsidiary of which the securities with voting rights are more than 50% owned by one parent.

Material — describes a fact to which a reasonable person would likely attach importance.

Officer — president, vice president, secretary, treasurer, principal financial officer and accounting officer, or any person performing these same functions, in an organization.

Parent — of a person is an affiliate that controls it either directly or indirectly.

Predecessor — a person that previously owned the majority portion of a business and assets before an acquisition.

Principal underwriter — the underwriter in privity of contract with the issuer.

Promoter — any person that takes initiative to found and organize an issue, or any person with a connection to the founding and organizing of an issue that receives more than 10% of the proceeds of the issue.

Prospectus — a prospectus that meets the requirements in section 10(a) of the Securities Act of 1933.

Registrant — issuer of securities that has filed for registration.

Seasoned issuer — an issuer that meets the requirements to file Form S-3 or F-3, but is not large enough to be considered a WKSI.

Share — a share of corporate stock or unit of interest in other types of organizations.

Shell company — a registrant other than an asset-backed issuer that has little-to-no operations and little-to-no assets.

Significant subsidiary — a subsidiary of a registrant that comprises more than 10% of the registrant's total assets.

Smaller reporting company — certain issuers that are not investment companies or asset-backed issuers and that have less than $75 million in public float.

Subsidiary — an affiliate control directly or indirectly by a specific person.

Succession — direct acquisition of assets by merger, consolidation, purchase, or other direct transfer.

Totally held subsidiary — a subsidiary that is owned 100% by its parent or its parents' other subsidiaries and is not significantly indebted to any other person.

Unseasoned reporting issuer - an issuer that is required to file reports as per the Exchange Act, but does not meet the eligibility requirements needed for Form S-3 or F-3.

Voting securities — securities that provide the owners with the right to vote on election of directors.

Well-known seasoned issuer — a status given by the SEC to certain well-known issuers that have a market value of $700 million or more.

Wholly owned subsidiary — a subsidiary, the outstanding voting securities of which are owned 100% by a parent or a parent's other wholly owned subsidiaries.

Written communication — any communication via written, printed, radio, television, or graphic media.

SEC RULE 415

To take advantage of the shelf registration rule, the issuer must register with the SEC with a prospectus. The rule allows issuers to register up to two years prior to the actual public offering. This allows the issuer flexibility in matching financial needs to market conditions.

Base prospectus - the original prospectus sent to the SEC with the registration that covers multiple offerings.

Prospectus supplement - the less detailed prospectus submitted when the issuer wants to make the offer public.

Refreshing requirements - sales of issues from a shelf registration are allowed for three years after the effective date of the registration, at which point a new registration statement would need to be filed if the issue desired to continue with the offering.

REGULATION D

Regulation D identifies what a private placement offering is, and outlines the rules governing private placements offerings that do not have to register. Regulation D is comprised of six rules - Rule 501, 502, 503, 504, 505, and 506.

RULE 501

Accredited investor - certain banks, certain private business development companies, and individuals with a net worth of more than $1,000,000 can be accredited investors, among others.

Affiliate - a person that directly or indirectly controls, or is controlled by, the stated person.

Aggregate offering price - total of all cash, services, property, notes, cancellation of debt, or other consideration that will be received by an issuer from the sale of the securities.

Business combination - when two or more businesses come together under common control, such as in an acquisition.

Calculation of number of purchasers - provides exclusions when calculating total number of investors under a Regulation D offering, including family members, and accredited investors.

Executive officer - any president or vice president of a functional division of a company, or other policy making persons.

Issuer - any person who issues securities.

Purchaser representative - a person capable of making financial decisions and has a written agreement with the purchaser to represent them.

RULE 502

Integration - securities that are sold six months before the beginning of, or six months after, the completion of a Regulation D offering are not part of the same offering (they are not *integrated*).

Information requirements - when a sale is made to a non-accredited investor, certain financial and non-financial information needs to be provided to the investor prior to sale.

Limitation on manner of offering - the issuer cannot advertise the offering via any form of general advertisement.

Limitations of resale - securities purchased via a Regulation D offering cannot be resold without being registered with the SEC.

RULE 503

Form D must be filed for new Regulation D offerings within 15 calendar days from the date of the first sale. An amendment to Form D can be filed at any time. An amendment to Form D must be filed to correct any material error or change in information.

RULE 504

Exemption - the registration exemption is extended to offerings as long as the issuer is not required to register, is not an investment company, and is not a company in development with no purpose or that plans to merge with another unidentified company.

Conditions to be met - the offering must meet the requirements in Rules 501 and 502.

Limitation of aggregate offering price - the aggregate offering price cannot exceed $1,000,000 less the price of all securities sold within the 12 months prior to the start of the Regulation D offering.

RULE 505

Exemption - the registration exemption is extended to offerings that are not investment companies

General conditions - the offering must meet the requirements in Rules 501 and 502.

Specific conditions - the aggregate offering price cannot exceed $5,000,000 less the price of all securities sold within the 12 months prior to the start of the Regulation D offering.

Limitation on number of purchasers - there can be no more than 35 purchasers

Disqualifications - an offering will be disqualified if the issuer is the subject of certain proceedings, examinations, refusal orders, and felony or misdemeanor convictions, among other things.

EXEMPTIONS

Exemption - the registration exemption is extended to issuers that satisfy the conditions, regardless of offering amount.

General conditions - the offering must meet the requirements in Rules 501 and 502.

Specific conditions - there is a limitation on the number of purchasers and the nature of purchasers.

1. Limitation on number of purchasers - there can be no more than 35 purchasers.
2. Nature of purchasers - each purchaser who is not an accredited investor must have knowledge and experience making him capable of evaluating the risks involved with the investment.

REGULATION S

General purpose - Regulation S states that securities bought and sold outside of the United States do not need to register with the SEC.

General conditions:

1. All transactions must be off-shore transactions.
2. Directed selling efforts may not be made in the United States.

Offshore transaction - a transaction that does not involve a United States person and meets one of the following criteria:

1. the buyer is outside of the United States
2. the transaction takes places on the trading floor of a foreign exchange
3. the transaction takes place via an offshore securities market

Substantial United States market interest (SUSMI)

1. Equity security - 1) the United States was the largest market in the previous year, 2) or the United States comprised 20% or more of all trading, and no foreign market comprised 55% or more of all trading.
2. Debt security - 1) there are 300 or more United States persons as investors, 2) at least $1 billion of the principal is owned by United States persons, or 3) at least 20% of the principal is owned by United States persons.

Directed selling efforts - any selling efforts that can be reasonably assumed to be targeting a United States market such as mailings in the United States, advertising in United States publications, and radio or TV advertisements broadcast in the United States.

Distributor - anyone who participates in the distribution of securities.

Offering restrictions:

1. Distributors agree 1) that any sales made during the distribution compliance period are compliant and 2) to not hedge transactions during the distribution compliance period.
2. All materials and documents must state that the security has not been registered according the Securities Act and cannot be bought or sold in the United States.

Distribution compliance period - the 40-day period during which an offer or sale relying on Regulation S is not made with any United States person to ensure the issuer is not engaging in unregistered trading in the United States.

United States person - any resident of the United States, any US partnership or corporation, any estate with an executor that is a United States person, any foreign agency in the United States, any discretionary or non-discretionary account of a United States person, and any foreign partnership or corporation created by a United States person with the purpose of investing in Regulation S securities (unless owned by accredited investors).

RULE 903

Rule 903 of Regulation S outlines three categories of issuer safe harbors. Category 1 offerings are offerings from foreign issuers with no SUSMI (substantial United States market interest) security being transacted, overseas directed offerings, offerings of securities backed by faith or credit of a foreign country, and certain employee benefit plans of foreign countries. Category 2 offerings are offerings of equity from foreign reporting issuers, offerings of debt from reporting issuers, and offerings of debt from non-reporting foreign issuers.

Additional requirements: each participant is required to implement offering restrictions, a 40-day distribution compliance period applies during which no United States person can be solicited, and distributors must inform participants that the distribution compliance period applies to them as well.

Category 3 offerings are offerings of equity from domestic issuers both reporting and non-reporting, offerings of equity non-reporting foreign issuers with SUSMI securities, and offerings of debt by non-reporting domestic issuers not under category 1.

Additional requirements for debt securities: a 40-day distribution compliance period applies during which no United States person can be solicited. During said compliance period, a temporary global security that cannot be exchanged with definite securities must be used until period expiration, and for a buyer that is a non-distributor, until it is certified that a non-United States person verifies beneficial ownership.

Additional requirements for equity securities: a one-year distribution compliance period applies during which no United States person can be solicited. During said compliance period, any purchaser must certify that he is a non-United States person. The purchaser must agree that any resale of the security will be according to Regulation S and that he will not hedge the securities.

RULE 904

The resale safe harbor allows for the resale by persons other than the issuer so long as the general conditions (offshore transactions and no directed selling) are met, as well as the addition requirements.

Additional requirements:

1. For the resale before expiration of compliance period - 1) the buyer cannot be a United States person, 2) the buyer cannot be a dealer and the seller has to send the buyer a notice that the securities can only be sold during the distribution compliance period pursuant to Regulation S.

2. For the resale by certain affiliates - officers or affiliates of the issuer or distributor who may resell securities under the resale safe harbor must not receive a fee or compensation of any kind other than the customary broker's commission.

RULE 144

Affiliate - an affiliate of an issuer is a person who either directly or through an intermediary controls or is under common control with an issuer.

Person - a person whose account securities are sold based on Rule 144 and include relatives, trusts or estates in which the person owns 10% or more, and legal organizations in which a person owns 10% or more of the equity.

Restricted Securities:

1. Securities directly acquired from issuer through means not involving a public offering.
2. Securities acquired from issuer that are subject to Rule 502(d) or 701(c).
3. Securities acquired via transactions subject to Rule 144A, Regulation CE, Rule 901 or 903, Rule 801 or 802, or section 4(5) of The Securities Act of 1933.

Debt securities:

1. Securities other than those defined in Rule 405.
2. Certain non-participatory preferred stock.
3. Asset-backed securities.

Rule 144 defines when a person is not engaged in distributing a security, and therefore not an underwriter as defined in Section 2(a)(11) of The Securities Act of 1933. It is the regulation governing the resale of securities by control persons.

Conditions to be met:

1. For non-affiliates - a person who has not been an affiliate for a period or three months prior to the sale of a security and sells restricted securities for his own benefit is not considered an underwriter.
2. For affiliates - a person who has been an affiliate of the issuer for a period of three months prior to the sale of a security and sells restricted securities for their own benefit is not considered an underwriter.

Current public information - the issuer has to have adequate public information available.

Holding period for restricted securities - when the issuer is subject to the reporting requirements in section 13 or 15(d) there must be a period of at least six months between the acquisition and resale of securities. This period extends to one year if the issuer is not subject to the reporting requirements in section 13 or 15(d).

Limitation on amount of securities sold:

1. Securities sold for the account of an affiliate cannot exceed the greatest of:
   a. 1% of the other units of the same class according to the issuer
   b. the average weekly volume of the trading of the security in national securities exchanges

c. the average weekly volume of trading of the security as according to an effective transaction reporting plan

2. Debt securities - cannot exceed either the greatest of the limitations in (e)(1) of Rule 144 (above) or 10% of the total principal amount of the securities issued.

REGULATION S-X

Regulation S-X contains regulations governing the content and format of financial statements in a registration, and covers statements including consolidated balance sheets, consolidated statements of income, changes in stockholders' equity and non-controlling interests, financial statements of business acquired or to be acquired, and separated financial statements of subsidiaries.

REGULATION S-K

Business - description of business; description of property; disclosure of any legal proceedings; and disclosure of mine safety.

Securities of registrant - market price of and dividends on common equity and related stock holder matters; and description of registrant securities.

Management and certain security holders - directors, executive officers, promoters and control persons; executive compensation, security ownership of certain beneficial owners and management; transactions with related persons, promoters and certain control persons; compliance with Section 16(a) of the Exchange Act, code of ethics; and corporate governance.

Registration statement and prospectus provisions - forepart of registration statement and outside front cover page of prospectus; inside front and outside back cover pages of prospectus; prospectus summary, risk factors, and ratio of earnings to fixed charges; use of proceeds; determination of offering price; dilution; selling security holders; plan of distribution; interests of named experts and counsel; disclosure of commission position on indemnification for Securities Act liabilities; other expenses of issuance and distribution; and undertakings.

Financial information - selected financial data; supplementary financial information; management's discussion and analysis of financial condition and results of operations; changes in and disagreements with accountants on accounting and financial disclosure; quantitative and qualitative disclosures about market risk; disclosure controls and procedures; and internal control over financial reporting.

Exhibits - exhibits.

Miscellaneous - recent sales of unregistered securities; use of proceeds from registered securities; and indemnification of directors and officers.

Roll-up transactions - individual partnership supplements; summary; risk factors and other considerations; comparative information; allocation of roll-up consideration; background of the roll-up transaction; reasons for, and alternatives to, the roll-up transaction; conflicts of interest; fairness of the transaction; reports, opinions and appraisals; source and amount of funds and transactional expenses; other provisions of the transaction; pro forma financial statements; and selected financial data.

REGULATION M-A AND FINRA RULE 5150

Regulation M-A - the SEC's detailed instructions and filing requirements for mergers and acquisitions.

Fairness opinions - fairness opinions are a professional opinion of the fairness of the terms of a proposed merger or acquisition. FINRA Rule 5150 outlines important disclosures that must be made in the fairness opinion, including any beneficial interest the preparer has in the transaction and material relationships the preparer has. It also outlines procedures that must be followed.

SEC RULE 100

ADTV — average daily trading volume during two full calendar months preceding.

At-the-market offering — offering of securities at a price other than a fixed price.

Independent bid — a bid from a person not a participant in the distribution of a security.

Penalty bid — an arrangement permitting the managing underwriter to reclaim selling concession from a syndicate member when securities sold are purchased in a syndicate covering transaction.

Public float — the outstanding amount of a security held by public investors.

Reference period — the two calendar months preceding the filing of a registration.

statement.

Restricted period — for securities with ADTV of $100,000 or more and a public float of $25 million or more, it is the period that begins one business day prior to determination of offering price or the date that the person begins to participate in the distribution, and ends when the person completed their participation.

Syndicate covering transaction — a purchase of a security for the sole distributor, to reduce a short position created in connection with an offering.

SEC RULES 101 AND 102 REGARDING ANTIMANIPULATION RULES IN REGULATION M

Illegal activities by distribution participants - it is illegal for distribution participants or affiliated purchasers to purchase a security while it is under the restricted period, with some exception.

Illegal activities by issuer and selling security holders during a distribution - it is illegal for issuers and selling security holders to purchase a security while it is under the restricted period, with some exceptions.

REGULATION FD

Adopted on August 15, 2000, Regulation FD (Fair Disclosure) is a set of rules with the purpose of addressing three insider trading issues: selective disclosure, insider trading liability, and family member or non-business relationship trades. Selective disclosure refers to when a securities issuer releases material nonpublic information, usually to certain industry professionals. The Regulation prohibits this without public disclosure of the information. The Regulation also states that insider trading liability (Rule 10b5-1) arises when an individual trades a security while aware of material nonpublic information. It provides for some exception when the individual can prove that the information was not a factor in the decision to trade. The Regulation also defines (Rule 10b5-2) how a family member - or an individual of another non-business relationship - can be liable for insider trading.

Prospectus in a registration statement after effective date (Rule 430B) - a prospectus filed with a registration statement can omit certain unknown or unavailable information.

SEC Rules 134, 135, and 135A

Rule 134 - factual information (name, address, phone number, etc.), security title and amount offered, a brief description of the issuer's type of business, the price of the security, maturity and interest rate provisions (fixed income security), brief description of intended use of proceeds, type of underwriting and names of underwriters, anticipated offering schedule, description of underwriting procedures, counsel's opinion that security is legal or exempt from certain taxes, whether security is offered through rights issued to security holders, statements required by state law, names of selling security holders, names of exchanges or markets, ticker symbol, CUSIP number, and information correcting previous inaccuracies.

Rule 135 - a notice of proposed registered offerings is not an offer to sell as long as it meets specific requirements.

Rule 135A - a generic advertisement that does not specify the name of a security or investment company is not an offer to sell as long as it meets specific requirements.

SEC Rules 137, 138, and 139

Rule 137 - a publication that is an opinion, report, or research from a broker/dealer who is not a participant in issue are allowed and not considered part of the definition of "offers," "participates," or "participation" as found in Section 2(11) of the Securities Act of 1933.

Rule 138 - a research publication from a broker/dealer who is a participant of an issue is allowed as long as the report is regarding the issuer's common stock or convertible debt securities and the issue involves only non-convertible debt securities, or as long as the report is regarding the non-convertible debt securities and the issue involves only common stock or convertible debt securities.

Rule 139 a broker/dealer can in certain situations publish recommendations for securities in which they are a participant such as when it is part of a report with similar information about numerous other similar issuers, the information is given no more prominence than that of other issuers, or is in the normal course of business.

SEC Rules 153A, 172, 174, and 460

When shareholders are entitled to receive prospectus - in transactions such as corporate reorganization, shareholders are entitled to receive a prospectus prior to voting on the issue (Rule 153A).

Rule 172 - exempts certain confirmations and notice of allocations from the prospectus delivery requirements when the registration statement is effective, the issuer has no Section 8A proceedings, and the issue has filed or will file a prospectus with the SEC.

Rule 174 - a prospectus must be delivered before or at time of confirmation. A prospectus need not be delivered if registration was filed on Form F-6 or in certain situations when the issuer is subject to filing requirements of Section 13 or 15(d) of the Securities Exchange Act of 1934.

Distribution to underwriters and dealers - issuers are to distribute a preliminary prospectus to each participating underwriter and dealer and their associated persons (SEC Rule 460 and 15c2-8).

SEC Rules 163, 163A, 168, and 169

Rule 163 - an offering by a WKSI (well-known seasoned issuer) before the registration effective date is exempt from the Section 5(c) prohibitions as long as certain requirements are met.

Rule 163A - any communication made more than 30 days before registration effective date is not an offer to sell as long as certain requirements are met.

Rule 168 - the regular release of factual or forward looking information as long as certain requirements are met.

Rule 169 - the regular release of factual business information is not an offer to sell as long as certain requirements are met.

SEC RULE 164

Rule 164 - provides for some leniency in the free writing prospectus requirements for certain offerings.

Conditions for WKSIs - A WKSI can use a free writing prospectus as long as a registration statement has been filed that includes a prospectus.

SEC RULES 254 AND 256

1. Sales of any kind are prohibited before qualification of the offering statement. Before the qualification, issuers and underwriters can attempt to measure the interest of a given security through the means of publications and broadcasts. However, all publications and broadcasts must contain phrasing explaining that it is not a solicitation of funds, that any funds sent in response will be denied, and that a statement of interest does not obligate the recipient to purchase the security later. Potential investors can send in their personal information to be contacted at a later date when the offer is qualified.
2. Seven copies or any advertisement or transcripts of any broadcast are to be filed with the SEC.
3. Rule 258 states that the SEC has the right to revoke temporarily any registration that is not complaint with Regulation A.

SECTION 10 OF THE SECURITIES ACT OF 1933 AND SEC RULES 427 AND 424

Information required in a prospectus (Section 10 of the Securities Act of 1933):

1. The information in the registration statement.
2. Nine months after the registration effective date, the information in the prospectus cannot be older than 16 months.

Contents of prospectuses after nine months of registration (Rule 427) - information can be left out as long as later information covering the same in included.

Number of copies to be filed (Rule 424) - five copies need to be filed with the SEC as part of the registration statement, and ten copies of Section 10 prospectuses.

SEC RULES 430, 430A, AND 430B

Prospectus for use prior to effective date (Rule 430) - prospectus can be used prior to effective date so long as all requirements are met.

Prospectus in a registration statement at time of effectiveness (Rule 430A)- a prospectus submitted as part of a registration statement can omit certain details so long as certain requirements are met, such as the securities only being offered for cash.

SEC Rule 433

Conditions for non-reporting and unseasoned issuers - if the issuer is to give compensation for the dissemination of the free writing prospectus, a registration statement has to have been previous filed that includes a prospectus. The free writing prospectus has to be accompanied by the original prospectus.

Written communication - written communication that is a road show is not required to be filed. A road show written communication does have to be filed if the offering is for common equity or convertible equities under an issuer that is not at the time required to file reports with the SEC, unless there is a bona fide electronic version of the road show made available.

Bona fide electronic road show - a written communication regarding the offering of a security transmitted graphically and that involves a presentation of members of management.

NASD Rule 2711

Investment banking department — any department or division that carries out investment banking services for a member.

Investment banking services — acting as an underwriter or financial adviser, participating in selling group, providing venture capital.

Member of a research analyst's household — any individual with the same principal residence as the analyst.

Public appearance — any conference call, seminar, etc., in front of 15 or more persons or in front of any media representatives.

Research analyst — any person responsible for preparation of a research report.

Research analyst account — any account in which a research analyst - or member of a research analyst's household - has a beneficial interest.

Research department — any department or division that responsible for preparing a research report for a member.

Research report — written communication that includes an analysis of securities and sufficient information to base an investment decision on.

Subject company — the company whose securities are the subject of a research report.

Restriction on relationship with research department - a research analyst may not be under control of the member's banking department, and no investment banking activity personnel may influence the compensation of the analyst. Only personnel in charge of research reports may review or approve reports. Non-research personnel can only review reports to verify factual information or discover conflicts of interest.

Restrictions on communications with the subject company - a member cannot submit a research report to the subject company before it is published, except for certain cases when portions can be sent to be reviewed for factual information or conflicts of interest. An analyst can alert the subject company that he will be changing the rating of its securities after the close of trading the day before it is announced. An analyst cannot participate in efforts to solicit business, including participating in road shows.

Restrictions on research analyst compensation - no bonuses can be paid based on investment banking transactions, and an analyst's compensation can be reviewed annually by a committee, but the committee is to not contain a member of the investment banking department.

Prohibition of promise of favorable research - favorable research can never be promised as consideration or inducement for business.

Restrictions on publishing research reports and public appearances; termination of coverage - members are restricted in certain situations from publishing research reports and public appearances. If a member is to terminate coverage of a company, he must give notice of this termination and make a final research report.

Restrictions on personal trading by research analysts - in most situations, research analysts are restricted from trading the subject security before the initial public offering, or during a period beginning 30 days before the publication of a research report and ending five days after.

Disclosure requirements - in research reports, research analysts must disclose: ownership and material conflicts of interest, receipt of compensation, if the analyst has a position as an officer or director of the subject company, meaning of ratings, distribution of ratings, price chart, price targets, and market making. Reference to the location of the disclosure has to be prominent on the front page of the report.

Supervisory procedures - each member must have written rules designed to achieve compliance with Rule 2711, and each year, a senior officer must attest that the rules have been adopted and implemented.

Prohibition of retaliation against research analysts - no one can retaliate, or threaten to retaliate, against a research analyst because of information in a report.

NYSE RULE 13

Auto ex order - initiates an automatic execution when entered into the system. Includes market orders, limit orders, cancel orders, among others.

Closing offset (CO) order - an order for execution at the close of trading, assuming there is an imbalance at that time.

Day order - expires at end of trading (4 PM Eastern Time).

Do not reduce (DNR) order - the price is not to be reduced according to the amount of the ordinary cash dividend on dividend date.

Do not ship (DNS) order - an order that is not to be shipped to another market. If in standard process the security should be shipped to another market, it will be cancelled.

Do not increase (DNI) order - the price is not to be increased according to the amount of the cash dividend on dividend date.

Limit "at-the-close" order - a limit order set for potential execution at the close of the market day.

Market order - an order to purchase a security at the most advantageous price.

Market "at-the-close" (MOC) orders - a market order set for execution at the close of the market day.

Market "on-the-open" (MOO) orders - a market order set for execution at the opening of the market day.

SOFT DOLLAR ARRANGEMENTS AND SECTIONS 3 AND 28(E) OF THE SEA

Soft dollar arrangements - a soft dollar arrangement is when a person exercising investment discretion over a client account takes commissions earned from transactions for the client, and directs them to a 3rd party for other services that benefit the client, but are not necessarily directed by the client.

Definition of "investment discretion" (Section 3(a)(35)) - a person exercises "investment discretion" when:

1. a person is authorized to determine what investments are to be purchased or sold in an account
2. a person makes decisions regarding what investments are to be bought or sold even though a different person is responsible
3. or when a person exercises influence regarding what investments are to be bought or sold in an account as the SEC makes a rule determining it is in the public interest

Research services in exchange for brokerage (Section 28(e)) - soft dollar arrangements are not prohibited, so long as the commission provided is determined to be reasonable in relation to the research services. A person exercising investment discretion is to disclose the policies and practices regarding soft dollar arrangements.

REGULATION AC

Regulation AC requires analysts to certify their reported views. Any publication must contain phrasing that states the opinion is that of only the analyst and that the analyst has received no compensation for his opinion.

DUE DILIGENCE OF A FINANCING PROPOSAL AND TYPES OF COVENANTS

Elements of due diligence of a financing proposal

1. Preliminary study
2. Letter of intent
3. General examination - industry data, operational data, management and employee relations, financial data, and research and product development and expansion
4. Legal examination
5. Commitment committee

Covenants

1. Bond
2. Indenture
3. Financial
4. Default

SEC RELEASE 34-42728

SEC release 34-42728 is an interpretive release discussing the use of electronic media.

Evidence of electronic delivery can be received by telephone.

An investor can give global consent to receive electronic documents electronically.

PDF documents are an acceptable means of delivering documents, so long as the provider assists the recipient to access the documents, if necessary, at no charge.

According to the envelope theory, any information published within close proximity or hyperlinked within close proximity on the internet can be considered to be sent "in the same envelope."

Website content - an issuer is responsible for information hyperlinked on his website if he was involved in its preparation, or if they endorse the content. While an issuer is registering its security, the issuer's website will be reviewed to detect any violations of securities laws.

Conduct of securities offerings via the internet

1. Public offerings - issuers cannot sell securities until the registration of said security is effective and broadcast offers cannot be made until delivery of final prospectus.
2. Private offerings - in order to prove that the reader is an accredited investor permitted to receive an offer, a "check the box" type acknowledgement would not be sufficient, but a username and password type system could be.

Series 24 Practice Test

1. An underwriter that assumes full responsibility and financial liability for an issue is involved in what type of underwriting commitment?

a. Fill or Kill
b. Firm commitment
c. Best efforts commitment
d. Stand by commitment

2. Which of the following persons would be restricted from the purchase of Company A's IPO?

    I. Bob, the brother in law of Company A's CFO
    II. Tina, an attorney that works with Company A on legal matters
    III. Rosa, Company A's tax accountant
    IV. Frank, an associated person of the firm underwriting the IPO

a. IV only
b. I, III, and IV only
c. II, III, and IV only
d. I, II, III, and IV

3. Which of the following is true regarding ERISA requirements?

    I. Plan assets must be kept separate from other company assets
    II. Plan participates must be notified in writing of any important plan changes such as changes in vesting schedule or plan benefits
    III. ERISA laws apply to both corporate and governmental plans
    IV. An employee that works at least 1,000 hours, has at least one year of service, and is 21 years or older must be covered in a plan if the company offers one

a. I and II only
b. I, II, and IV only
c. I, II, and III only
d. I, II, III, and IV

4. All of the following are true regarding the Uniform Gifts to Minors Act except:

a. All securities in the UGMA account must be registered in the custodian's name
b. Only a parent or legal guardian may establish an UGMA account for their child, though anyone may contribute to it
c. The custodian of the UGMA account is entitled to reimbursement of expenses associated with managing the account
d. Minors are not allowed to trade in the account

5. The PATRIOT Act, at a minimum, requires firms and financial institutions to do which of the following?

    I. Verify and obtain customer information
    II. Establish, in writing, anti-money laundering procedures
    III. Provide employee training in anti-money laundering procedures
    IV. Report any suspicious activity to appropriate authorities within 30 days of observation

    a. I only
    b. I, II, and IV only
    c. I, II, and III only
    d. I, II, III, and IV

6. The Federal Telephone Consumer Protection Act of 1991 limits unsolicited calls to:

    a. The hours of 8:00 a.m. to 9:00 p.m.
    b. The hours of 7:00 a.m. to 8:00 p.m.
    c. The hours of 9:00 a.m. to 8:00 p.m.
    d. The hours of 7:30 a.m. to 7:30 p.m.

7. Jim and Judy want to open a brokerage account together in which Jim has ownership over only 20% of the account, with Judy having ownership and authority over the remainder. What type of account is best for Jim and Judy to open?

    a. Tenancy in Common
    b. Joint Tenancy with Right of Survivorship
    c. Transfer on Death Account
    d. They should each open separate accounts

8. The NYSE may delist a stock or company under certain circumstances, including which of the following?

    I. Publicly held shares fall below 600,000
    II. Pretax earnings for the previous 3 years have decreased to an average of less than $600,000
    III. Company files bankruptcy
    IV. Company fails to meet debt obligations

    a. I and II only
    b. II and III only
    c. III only
    d. I, II, III, and IV

9. All of the following are requirements for a stock or company to be listed on the NYSE except:

    a. There must be a national public interest for ownership and trading in the company
    b. There must be a minimum of 1,100,000 publicly held shares
    c. The company must have pre-tax earnings in the previous year of at least $5,000,000
    d. The company has at least 2,000 shareholders, each holding at least 100 common shares

10. Wendy has a lot of money that she would like to ensure is covered under SIPC rules. In order to maximize SIPC coverage, she opens various types of accounts, including a trust account. Which of the following best describes the SIPC coverage of the trust account?

a. The trust account will not be covered by SIPC, because trust accounts are never covered
b. The trust account will be covered by SIPC, because it is a qualifying trust account
c. The trust account may be covered by SIPC, depending upon the amount that is placed in the trust
d. The trust account will not be covered by SIPC, because it is not considered a qualified trust account

11. NYSE Rule 78 states which of the following about trading?

a. Firms are prohibited from pre-arranged trades, regardless of circumstances
b. Firms are prohibited from crossing orders within their own firm, regardless of circumstances
c. Firms may pre arrange trades, as long as there is full and written disclosure
d. Firms are prohibited from holding both a buy and sell order on the same security for different clients

12. NYSE Rule 61 requires that trades be made in round lots. Round lots are considered to be:

    I. 10 shares of listed stocks
    II. 100 shares of listed stocks
    III. $1,000 face amount of listed bonds
    IV. $10,000 face amount of listed bonds

a. I and III
b. II and III
c. I and IV
d. II and IV

13. An issuer would like to take advantage of Rule 415 of the Securities Act of 1933, regarding shelf registration. All of the following are true regarding the Rule except:

a. Issuer may register a new issue up to 2 year prior to the public offering
b. The rule is advantageous to issuers by allowing them to release a new issue when market conditions provide the most favorable outcomes
c. Once an issuer decides to issue the offering, it must notify the SEC within 2 days prior to release
d. Only one prospectus need be filed and submitted

14. Rule 134 allows issuers to distribute information about an issue to the public during the 20 day cooling off period. All of the following details can be included in the information except:

a. Date of offering
b. Type of security being offered
c. Size of the offering
d. Names of the underwriters

15. Rule 137 permits broker-dealers that are not part of the underwriting syndicate of a new issue to distribute which of the following?

    I. Reports on the issue
    II. Research on the issue
    III. Advertisements on the issue
    IV. Opinions on the issue

  a. I and II only
  b. I, II, and IV only
  c. I, II, and III only
  d. I, II, III, and IV

16. Order tickets must contain which of the following information?

    I. Security name
    II. Number of shares to be bought or sold
    III. Registered representative's information
    IV. Registered representative's manager's signature

  a. I and II only
  b. I, II, and III only
  c. I, II, and IV only
  d. I, II, III, and IV

17. All of the following are true regarding the abuse of insider information except:

  a. Firms are required to set up written procedures designed to prevent use of insider information
  b. A person who violates insider trading rules may be accountable for up to five times any resulting profit
  c. A firm that knowingly overlooks inappropriate insider trading may be assessed $1,000,000, or three times any resulting profit
  d. A reward of up to 10% of recovered amounts may be awarded to a reporter of illegal insider trading

18. In an over the counter trade, a Subject Quote is one in which:

  a. The quote may be changed upon confirmation
  b. The quote is the current price
  c. The quote is an estimate
  d. The quote is firm

19. For a small cap security to initially meet listing requirements for the NASDAQ, it must meet which of the following?

    I. Equity of $5,000,000
    II. Market cap of $50,000,000
    III. Pre-tax income of $750,000
    IV. Equity of $10,000,000

  a. Either I, II, or III
  b. Either I and II, or IV
  c. I, II, and IV
  d. I, II, and III

20. FINRA Rule 6541 protects customer limit orders by:

   a. Disallowing firms from placing limit orders for customers
   b. Ruling that customer limit orders must be placed ahead of the firm's limit orders
   c. Disallowing firms from placing their own limit orders
   d. Ruling that a firm's limit orders must be placed ahead of the customer's limit orders

21. Specialists play an important role in the markets by:

     I. Providing the market with liquidity
    II. Minimizing gaps between supply and demand
   III. Helping to provide price continuity
   IV. Maintaining a fair market

   a. I only
   b. II and III only
   c. II, III, and IV only
   d. I, II, III, and IV

22. According to Rules 17 A-3 and 17A-4, which of the following records must be maintained by a corporation for the entire life of the firm?

   a. General ledgers
   b. Board meeting minutes
   c. Copies of memos
   d. Order tickets

23. Tom, a registered representative, wants to open an investment account at another firm. Which of the following is true?

   a. Tom is not permitted to open an account at another firm
   b. Tom must receive prior written approval from his member firm before opening the account at the receiving firm
   c. Tom must disclose to the receiving firm his employment with the member firm
   d. The receiving firm should not honor such a request and should notify Tom's employer of his attempt

24. A firm filing bankruptcy must submit which of the following forms to the SEC to report such information?

   a. Fiscal year balance sheet
   b. Last year's tax return
   c. Form 8-K
   d. Form 10-K

25. Which of the following is true regarding a firm's fidelity bonds?

   a. Coverage requirements for a firm increase as net capital of the firm increases
   b. Coverage requirements are the same for each firm
   c. Once set, coverage requirements for a firm remain in place for the life of the firm
   d. Each firm must have coverage equal to 100% of the firm's net capital

26. Which of the following is most accurate regarding the FINRA manual?

a. It must be given to all customers at account opening
b. It must be made available to customers upon request
c. It must be given to all customers within 30 days of account opening
d. It is not required to be made available to customers, only to registered representatives and member firms

27. All of the following are true regarding arbitration except:

a. It is a more cost efficient method than litigation
b. It is required to settle disputes between two member firms
c. Decisions from arbitrated cases may be appealed
d. It is required to settle disputes between a member firm and clearing agency

28. Net asset value of an open end fund can be calculated as:

a. Previous day's closing price / Total market value
b. Previous day's total market value / Previous day's closing price
c. Number of shares in fund / Total market value
d. Total market value / Number of shares in fund

29. Based on FINRA rules, the sale of a mutual fund may not require a sales charge which exceeds:

a. 5.75% of the POP
b. 6.25% of the POP
c. 8.5% of the POP
d. 10% of the POP

30. All of the following are true regarding variable annuities except:

a. They are more susceptible to inflation than fixed annuities
b. The value of the annuity is based on the value of the underlying securities it holds
c. Compared with fixed annuities, variable annuities are more likely to produce capital gains
d. Payouts of the annuity will be based on the value of the underlying securities

31. Nicole wants to short sale a stock, which is currently trading at $3. Which of the following is true regarding her options to short sell?

a. Short selling stocks trading under $5 is not permitted
b. Her minimum margin will be set at 100% of the value of the sale
c. The minimum margin for stocks trading under $5 is set at $2.50 per share
d. Firms encourage the short selling of stocks under $5, to help provide trading volume

32. Which of the following trade flat, or without accrued interest?

I. Income bonds
II. Treasury bonds
III. Commercial paper
IV. Zero Coupon bonds

a. I and IV only
b. II, III, and IV only
c. III and IV only
d. I, II, III, and IV

33. All of the following are true regarding a member wishing to resign except:

a. Members must submit written notice to FINRA, informing of resignation
b. Members must have no complaints against them at the time of resignation
c. Resignations become effective immediately after received by FINRA
d. Resigned members will be under FINRA jurisdiction for 2 years following resignation

34. All of the following are true regarding Forms U-4 and U-5 except:

a. A copy of the Form U-5 must be given to member upon termination
b. Form U-5 must be submitted to FINRA immediately upon member's resignation
c. Form U-4 must be modified and updated to reflect changes in member's information
d. Form U-5 must be provided upon request to potential new employer firms

35. All of the following are true regarding a security's ex-date except

a. The ex-date is the date on which a security is sold without a previously declared dividend
b. Exchanges set the ex-date as 2 days before the record date
c. The ex-date is the date on which the issuing company declares the dividend
d. An investor that purchases the stock after the ex-date will not receive the dividend

36. All of the following are true regarding Coverdell Education accounts except

a. The maximum contribution is $2,000 per year, per student
b. Withdrawals made for purposes other than qualified tuition will be penalized at a 10% rate
c. Contributions to the account are tax deductible in the year contributions are made
d. Funds may be used for qualified education expenses, including both elementary and secondary education

37. A traditional IRA:

    I. Has mandatory minimum distributions starting at age 59 1/2
    II. May no longer accept contributions to the account after the account holder reaches age 70 1/2
    III. Imposes a 10% penalty for early withdrawal of funds, if no qualified exception is met
    IV. Defers income tax and capital gains until funds are withdrawn

a. II and III only
b. I and II only
c. II, III, and IV only
d. I, II, III, and IV

38. Rule 254 of Regulation A details the requirements of the solicitation of interest in a security before an offering statement has been distributed. Which of the following is accurate regarding the rule?

I. Interested investors in the security may provide their name, phone number, and address as contact information
II. Issuers may only gauge interest in the upcoming security, but may not pre-sell
III. Disclosure must be given to interested investors stating that money is not being solicited
IV. Investors that indicate an interest in the security are obligated to purchase it.

a. I and II only
b. I, II, and III only
c. IV only
d. I, II, III, and IV

39. Rule 144 of the Securities and Exchange Act of 1933 discusses the conditions that must be met for a stockholder to sell their restricted securities. Conditions include

I. If the trade involves over 5000 shares or $50,000 in a three month period, the SEC must be notified
II. If sales occur three months after filing with the SEC, an amendment must also be submitted
III. The broker must not receive additional compensation exceeding their normal commission
IV. The trading volume formula must be applied to any restricted shares sold publicly

a. I and II only
b. I, II, and III only
c. I, II, and IV only
d. I, II, III, and IV

40. Securities that are sold outside the U.S. to non U.S. residents are exempt from SEC registration based on

a. Regulation S
b. Regulation T
c. Regulation A
d. Regulation D

41. According to Rules 137 and 138 of the Securities and Exchange Act of 1933, which of the following is true regarding underwriters?

a. Firms in an underwriting group are prohibited from recommending the purchase of an offer they are underwriting during the cooling-off period
b. Firms in an underwriting group are permitted to recommend the purchase of an offer they are underwriting during the cooling-off period
c. Firms in an underwriting group are permitted to recommend the purchase of a security that can be converted into one being underwritten
d. Underwriting firms cannot recommend issues that are not part of their underwriting and are not convertible into one of their underwritings

42. Company A and Company B are planning a merger, in which existing shareholders of Company A will receive shares of the newly merged company. Which of the following is true?

a. No new registration is needed, as long as Company A and Company B are both currently registered with the SEC
b. New registration is required since one security will be substituted for another
c. No new registration is needed because the two companies are merging, not reorganizing
d. No new registration is needed, though a Form 8-K must be filed with the SEC notifying the public of such changes

43. Which of the following is true regarding day trading by a noninstitutional customer?

I. Such customer must be given disclosure regarding risks and fees associated with day trading
II. Day trading is defined as participating in more than 4 trades in 5 days
III. Representatives must evaluate the suitability of a day trader including their income, net worth and investment objectives
IV. Representatives must approve in advance each trade placed by noninstitutional day trading customers

a. I only
b. I and II only
c. I, II, and III only
d. I, II, III, and IV

44. Which of the following are considered exclusions to the classification of an Investment Adviser under the Investment Advisers Act of 1940?

I. Those giving advice solely to family and friends
II. A bank holding company
III. Those advising only on government securities
IV. Those receiving only minimal compensation for advice related to securities

a. II and III only
b. I and IV only
c. II, III, and IV only
d. I, II, III, and IV

45. The Investment Advisers Act of 1940 creates regulations for investment advisory contracts, which state that

a. Investment advisory contracts may be oral or written
b. Contracts cannot contain provisions which allow an adviser to receive compensation based on capital gains in a client's account
c. Investment advisers are limited to $5,000 of compensation per customer account in any 12 month period
d. An adviser may include a provision in the contract to reduce fees if the account does not perform as well as anticipated

46. Initial margin requirements, based on Regulation T, are set at _____ for long positions of stocks and convertibles; _____ for short positions of stocks and convertibles; and _____ for corporate bonds.

a. 30%, 50% and 50%
b. 50%, 30% and 50%
c. 50%, 50% and 0%
d. 30%, 30% and 30%

47. FINRA member dues imposed annually are _____ per branch and _____ per registered person.

a. $75, $75
b. $50, $50
c. $1,000, $100
d. $1,000, $500

48. Once a firm becomes a FINRA member firm, it must meet which of the following requirements to maintain its membership?

I. Pay annual fees and dues
II. Create an Office of Supervisory Jurisdiction
III. Properly use the FINRA name
IV. Observe branch location regulations

a. I and III only
b. II and III only
c. I, II, and III only
d. I, II, III, and IV

49. Which of the following is true regarding member firms branches located within a bank?

I. The member firm must clearly identify and display the firm's name
II. Offices of the member firm must be distinct and separated from other bank spaces
III. Branches must disclose that member firms' accounts are not FDIC insured
IV. Member firms are not permitted to be located within a bank

a. I and III only
b. I, II, and III only
c. I and II only
d. IV only

50. In order to ensure timely and accurate reporting of quotations in the OTC market, FINRA requires market makers report NASDAQ trades how quickly after execution?

a. Immediately in real time
b. 10 seconds
c. 1 minute
d. 90 seconds

Answer Key and Explanations

1. B: An underwriter may participate in an issue by agreeing to a variety of different commitments. A Firm Commitment means the underwriter assumes the role of principal, purchases all of the securities, and is then responsible for selling such securities to the public. The financial liability of such a commitment lies with the underwriter. Best effort implies that the underwriter will try, though not guarantee, to fill all orders but is not liable for any that are unfilled. A stand by commitment means the underwriter is ready to purchase any remaining shares if the offer is undersubscribed. Fill or Kill is a type of brokerage order.

2. D: FINRA restricts insiders from involvement in a company's IPO, the initial public offering of company stock. An insider can generally be defined as anyone that has special, non public information about the company. This includes officers and employees of the company, as well as family members and other associated persons. In the case of Company A, all persons would be considered to have inside information about the company, and would be restricted by FINRA from purchasing shares of the company's IPO.

3. B: ERISA applies to corporate plans only. It does not apply to Federal or State government plans or employees. ERISA was established to protect plan participants and their assets. It also sets non discrimination standards and requires clear and necessary communication and disclosure to plan participants.

4. B: Any adult may establish and contribute to a minor's UGMA account, not just the parent or legal guardian. It is correct that all securities in the UGMA account must be registered in the custodian's name, the custodian of the UGMA account is entitled to reimbursement of expenses associated with managing the account, and that minors are not allowed to trade in the account. UGMA laws will vary from state to state.

5. D: The PATRIOT Act was created after September 11th as an effort for firms and financial institutions to help intercept and prevent terrorist activities. The Act requires that firms establish, in writing, procedures for anti-money laundering practices and train employees in such procedures. Any suspicious activity must be reported within 30 days of observation. The Act also requires institutions to obtain and verify proper identification from its customers.

6. A: The Federal Telephone Consumer Protection Act of 1991 limits unsolicited calls to the hours of 8:00 a.m. to 9:00 p.m. When unsolicited calls are placed, the caller is required by the Act to identify him or herself, their firm, and phone number. A popular provision of the Act allows consumers to request placement on the do not call list to avoid unsolicited calls.

7. A: With unequal ownership, it is best for Jim and Judy to open a Tenancy in Common account. This account will allow them to have joint ownership, but in their respective ownership amounts only. In this case, Jim will have ownership only on his 20% and Judy only on her 80%. This is in contrast to an account titled Joint Tenants with Right of Survivorship, in which each owner has an equal and undivided interest in the entire account. Single accounts could solve the problem, but the questions states that Jim and Judy would like to open a joint account.

8. D: Though rare, the NYSE can and may delist a company or stock based on certain requirements not being met. Such circumstances include all of the above mentioned reasons along with the following: number of shareholders with over 100 shares drops below 1,200; aggregate market value of stock is less than $12,000,000 and an aggregate market value of publicly held shares falls below $8,000,000; companies that reduce their operations, issue non-voting common stock, fail to maintain healthy accounting practices, fail to make adequate public disclosures or fail to solicit proxies.

9. C: The company must have pre-tax earnings in the previous year of $2,500,000 as a requirement of listing on the NYSE. To maintain their listing, earnings for the previous 3 years should be at least an average of $600,000. The other answer choices are all necessary requirements for NYSE listing.

10. D: While trust accounts may qualify for SIPC coverage, this particular trust will not be considered a "qualifying" trust account because the information states that Wendy opened the trust specifically to obtain additional SIPC coverage. A trust is considered qualified for SIPC purposes if it is a valid trust created by written instrument, and not created for the purpose of additional coverage.

11. A: NYSE Rule 78 prohibits prearranged trading by a firm (regardless of disclosure) because such a practice is considered market manipulation. Firms are not prohibited from holding both a buy and sell order on the same security for different clients. However, Rule 76 states that these orders may not be crossed within their own firm without first being offered in the trading market.

12. B: Round lots are in the form of 100 shares of listed stock, or $1,000 face value of listed bonds, as stated by NYSE Rule 61. Quotations on odd lots are allowed but must include the specific number of shares the quote covers.

13. D: Rule 415 allows the issuer to register a new issue up to 2 years prior to the public offering. This could be advantageous to issuers by allowing them to release a new issue when market conditions provide the most favorable outcomes. Once an issuer decides to issue the offering, it must notify the SEC at least 2 days prior to release. The rule requires that issuers file an initial prospectus that covers multiple offerings. However, when the issue is taken to the public, a new supplemental prospectus must be submitted.

14. A: Rule 134 allows issuers to distribute information about an issue to the public during the 20 day cooling-off period. Details which may be reported include the name and type of business of the issuer, the type of security being offered, size of the offering, POP and names of the underwriters. In addition, it may also give an estimated offering schedule, though an exact date may not be given. Other information may include what exchange the issue is expected to trade on and the anticipated purpose of the proceeds being collected.

15. B: Rule 137 permits broker dealers that are not part of the underwriting syndicate of a new issue to distribute reports, research and opinions on the issue. The rule prohibits, however, such broker dealers to be hired by the underwriting group to distribute such information.

16. D: A valid order ticket must include the following information: whether the customer is taking a long or short position, the number of shares to be bought or sold, identification of the security, duration of the order, price of execution, name and account number of customer, registered representative's information and registered representative's manager's signature.

17. B: Insider trading rules help broker dealers maintain appropriate procedures to combat illegal insider trading. Firms are required to set up written procedures, designed as "Chinese walls," to prevent important insider information from being leaked to unnecessary individuals. If a firm knowingly overlooks inappropriate insider trading, it may be assessed $1,000,000, or three times any resulting profit. Individuals who violate insider trading rules may be accountable for up to three times any resulting profit, known as treble damages. As an incentive, a reward of up to 10% of recovered amounts may be awarded to anyone reporting illegal insider trading.

18. A: A Subject Quote is one that may be subject to change upon confirmation. If this type of trade is made, the dealer must specify it is a subject quote upon submission. A quote which a dealer believes is the current price is called a nominal quote. If the quote is an estimate of the price at which the dealer will trade, this is known as a workout quote. And lastly, a firm quote is the price at which the market maker will trade.

19. A: For a small cap security to initially meet listing requirements for the NASDAQ, it must meet any of the three following requirements: equity of $5,000,000, a market cap of $50,000,000, or pre-tax income of $750,000. Equity of $10,000,000 is required for large cap stocks. Keep in mind that initial listing requirements differ from the minimum requirements a company must maintain in order to remain listed on an exchange.

20. B: FINRA Rule 6541 protects customer limit orders by requiring customer limit orders to be placed ahead of the firm's limit orders, giving priority to the public. In this way, a firm may not trade ahead of its customers at a price that is the same or better for the same security. It does not prohibit limit orders from being placed for the firm or customers.

21. D: Specialists, who must be registered as such with the Exchange, help to make markets efficient (and thereby liquid and fair) by minimizing gaps between supply and demand and helping to provide price continuity. They do this by maintaining their own accounts, which they can then use to meet customer needs if and when the market cannot meet these needs itself. NYSE Rule 103 and 104 regulate who may act as a specialist on the floor, and defines their respective responsibilities and roles.

22. B: Rules 17-A-3 and 17 A-4 is related to record keeping of broker-dealers. Records that must be maintained by the firm for its entire existence include its Articles of Incorporation, board meeting minutes, and partnership agreements. Other records are required to be held for defined periods of either three or six years. Copies of memos and order tickets are examples of items that may be held for a period of three years, while general ledgers must be held for six.

23. C: Tom is permitted to open an account at another firm; however, he must disclose his employment association with his current firm to the receiving firm. The receiving firm must submit information to his employer firm upon request and must also monitor the account to ensure no trades are being placed which may harm his employer's firm. Prior written approval for account opening is not necessary.

24. C: Form 8-K is used by corporations to report major events to the SEC. This allows fair and timely disclosure of such events to shareholders and to the public. In the event a company files bankruptcy, this must be reported. Form 10-K is the annual report that must be filed by corporations to the SEC.

25. A: FINRA requires all firms to maintain fidelity bonds on employees to protect against losses caused by theft, misuse of funds, or other fraudulent acts. The bonds serve as a type of insurance for investors and companies. The amount of coverage required by FINRA to be maintained by each firm varies depending upon the net capital of the firm. Coverage requirements increase as the firm's net capital increases. In general, coverage requirements are 120% of the firm's net capital. Coverage is reviewed annually to ensure the company is maintaining adequate coverage.

26. B: FINRA rules require that each member firm make available the FINRA manual upon customer request. Thus, each member firm must keep a copy in their office. It is unnecessary to distribute copies of the manual upon account opening, or any other time, other than at the customer's request to view.

27. C: Because it is a more cost efficient method than litigation, arbitration is required to settle disputes between two member firms as well as to settle disputes between a member firm and a clearing agency. It may or may not be used to settle customer disputes. Decisions from arbitrated cases cannot be appealed.

28. D: Net asset value of a fund is calculated by taking the total market value of the fund and dividing it by the fund's total number of shares. It is calculated daily, based on the closing price of the fund.

29. C: Sales charges on mutual funds may not exceed 8.5% of the POP, based on FINRA rules. If the firm doesn't offer dividend reinvestment, the maximum sales charge decreases to 7.25%. If it doesn't offer rights of accumulation, the maximum sales charge is 8%, and if the firm offers neither dividend reinvestment nor rights of accumulation, the maximum charge is 6.75%.

30. A: The value of the annuity and its payout is based on the value of the underlying securities it holds. Since variable annuities hold equities as the underlying investment, they are more likely to produce capital gains. They are also less susceptible to changes in inflation compared to fixed annuities.

31. B: Nicole may short sell a stock that is valued under $5; however additional margin rules apply for such securities. For stocks under $5, the minimum margin will be set at either the greater of $2.50 per share, or 100% of the stock's value. In Nicole's case, minimum margin will be set at 100%. Firms discourage the short selling of low-priced stocks because of the additional risks.

32. D: Usually, when a bond trade settles, the bond buyer must pay the seller the purchase price of the bond and any accrued interest. Accrued interest is money earned on the bond that has accrued between the last interest payment date and the trade settlement date. There is no accrued interest with income bonds, treasury bills, commercial paper, and zero coupon bonds.

33. C: A member wishing to resign may voluntarily do so by submitting written notice to FINRA. The member must have no complaints against them at the time of resignation, or owe any money to FINRA. Resignation does not become effective until 30 days after notice and resigned members will be under FINRA jurisdiction for 2 years following resignation.

34. B: Form U-4 is used by individuals wishing to register with FINRA and contains important personal and historical information on the individual. It must be updated with changes made to the individual's information, as necessary. Form U-5 is used upon termination of an employee. The form must be submitted within 30 days of termination, and a copy of this form must be given to the terminated employee. If the terminated employee wishes to obtain employment at another member firm, it must provide a copy of the Form U-5 upon request.

35. C: The date on which the issuing company declares the dividend is called the declaration date, not the ex-date. The ex-date is the date on which a security is sold without a previously declared dividend. An investor that purchases the stock after the ex-date will not receive the dividend. Exchanges set the ex-date as 2 days before the record date.

36. C: Coverdell Education accounts are education savings accounts set up for the benefit of a beneficiary, which provide tax deferral when funds are used for qualified tuition expenses. Qualified tuition expenses include both elementary and secondary education costs. If funds are used for expenses other than these, a 10% penalty is imposed. Contributions to the account are not tax deductible, though they do grow tax deferred. Anyone may open a Coverdell, though the maximum contribution limit is $2,000 per beneficiary per year.

37. C: A traditional IRA is a retirement savings vehicle which offers investors the benefit of tax deferral on income tax and capital gains until funds are withdrawn in retirement. Contributions can not be made after the account holder reaches age 70 ½, at which point mandatory distributions must begin. At age 59 ½, an account holder may choose to distribute funds without the 10% penalty for early withdrawal.

38. B: Rule 254 of Regulation A details the requirements of the solicitation of interest in a security before an offering statement has been distributed. Issuers may only gauge interest in the upcoming security and are not permitted to sell. Interested investors in the security may provide their name, number, and address as contact information. In return, such investors must receive disclosure which states that no money is being solicited and that there is no obligation to purchase the security at time of issue.

39. D: Rule 144 of the Securities and Exchange Act of 1933 discusses the conditions that must be met for a stockholder to sell their restricted securities. Such conditions include the following; If the trade involves over 5000 shares or $50,000 in a three month period, the SEC must be notified, if sales occur after a three month period of filing with the SEC, an amendment must also be submitted, the broker must not receive additional compensation which exceeds their normal commission, and the trading volume formula must be applied to any restricted shares sold publicly. Rule 144 attempts to simplify the sale process of restricted stock in small quantities.

40. A: Securities that are sold outside the U.S. to non-U.S. residents are exempt from SEC registration based on Regulation S. Regulation S securities are considered restricted because they are only available for sale to specific individuals. Regulation T deals with margin trading, Regulation A deals with small issue exemptions, and Regulation D deals with private placement offerings.

41. A: According to Rule 137, firms in an underwriting group are prohibited from recommending the purchase of an offer they are underwriting during the cooling-off period. They are also prohibited from recommending the purchase of a security that can be converted into one being underwritten. Rule 138 however, permits underwriting firms to recommend issues that are not part of their underwriting and are not convertible into one of their underwritings.

42. B: According to Rule 145 of the Securities and Exchange Act of 1933, new registration is required since one security will be substituted for another. Rule 145 details registration protocol for mergers and reorganization of a company. The rule protects investors from unnecessary confusion regarding company changes.

43. C: Day trading by a non-institutional customer requires additional information, monitoring and disclosure by a registered representative. Day trading is defined as participating in more than 4 trades in 5 days. Such customers must be given disclosures regarding the risks and fees associated with day trading, including profits earned by the firm from commissions on trading. Representatives must evaluate the suitability of a day trader including their income, net worth, investment objective, marital status, age, tax status, and previous trading experience.

44. A: The Investment and Advisers Act of 1940 classifies who is considered an Investment Adviser under the Act and who is considered exempt. Among those exempt are bank holding companies and anyone advising only on government securities. In addition, professionals whose advisory services are incidental to their job role, securities professionals who do not receive compensation for their advice, and persons who publish mass media are also exempt.

45. B: The Investment Advisers Act of 1940 creates regulations for investment advisory contracts and states that contracts cannot contain provisions allowing an adviser to receive compensation based on capital gains in a client's account. Similarly, contracts may not include a provision to reduce fees if the account does not perform as well as anticipated. The contract must be written.

46. C: Initial margin requirements, based on Regulation T, are set at 50% for long positions of stocks and convertibles and 50% for short positions of stocks and convertibles. Government municipal bonds and corporate bonds are not subject to initial margin requirements.

47. A: FINRA charges dues annually. These dues are set at $75 per branch and $75 per registered person.

48. D: Once a firm becomes a FINRA member firm, it must pay annual fees and dues, create an Office of Supervisory Jurisdiction, properly use the FINRA name, and observe branch location regulations in order to maintain its membership.

49. B: FINRA member firms may have branches located within a bank if certain conditions and precautions are met. The member firm must clearly identify and display the firm's name and offices of the member firm must be distinct and separated from other bank spaces. In addition, branches must disclose that member firms' accounts are not FDIC insured and are subject to risk.

50. B: In order to ensure timely and accurate reporting of quotations in the OTC market, FINRA requires market makers to report NASDAQ trades within 10 seconds after execution. This is known as the 10-second report rule and applies to all trades made within the normal trading day. If trades occur outside that time, notification must be given at the beginning of the next trading day. The rule previously required reporting within 30 seconds, and 90 seconds before that.

How to Overcome Test Anxiety

Just the thought of taking a test is enough to make most people a little nervous. A test is an important event that can have a long-term impact on your future, so it's important to take it seriously and it's natural to feel anxious about performing well. But just because anxiety is normal, that doesn't mean that it's helpful in test taking, or that you should simply accept it as part of your life. Anxiety can have a variety of effects. These effects can be mild, like making you feel slightly nervous, or severe, like blocking your ability to focus or remember even a simple detail.

If you experience test anxiety—whether severe or mild—it's important to know how to beat it. To discover this, first you need to understand what causes test anxiety.

Causes of Test Anxiety

While we often think of anxiety as an uncontrollable emotional state, it can actually be caused by simple, practical things. One of the most common causes of test anxiety is that a person does not feel adequately prepared for their test. This feeling can be the result of many different issues such as poor study habits or lack of organization, but the most common culprit is time management. Starting to study too late, failing to organize your study time to cover all of the material, or being distracted while you study will mean that you're not well prepared for the test. This may lead to cramming the night before, which will cause you to be physically and mentally exhausted for the test. Poor time management also contributes to feelings of stress, fear, and hopelessness as you realize you are not well prepared but don't know what to do about it.

Other times, test anxiety is not related to your preparation for the test but comes from unresolved fear. This may be a past failure on a test, or poor performance on tests in general. It may come from comparing yourself to others who seem to be performing better or from the stress of living up to expectations. Anxiety may be driven by fears of the future—how failure on this test would affect your educational and career goals. These fears are often completely irrational, but they can still negatively impact your test performance.

> **Review Video: <u>3 Reasons You Have Test Anxiety</u>**
> Visit mometrix.com/academy and enter code: 428468

Elements of Test Anxiety

As mentioned earlier, test anxiety is considered to be an emotional state, but it has physical and mental components as well. Sometimes you may not even realize that you are suffering from test anxiety until you notice the physical symptoms. These can include trembling hands, rapid heartbeat, sweating, nausea, and tense muscles. Extreme anxiety may lead to fainting or vomiting. Obviously, any of these symptoms can have a negative impact on testing. It is important to recognize them as soon as they begin to occur so that you can address the problem before it damages your performance.

Review Video: 3 Ways to Tell You Have Test Anxiety
Visit mometrix.com/academy and enter code: 927847

The mental components of test anxiety include trouble focusing and inability to remember learned information. During a test, your mind is on high alert, which can help you recall information and stay focused for an extended period of time. However, anxiety interferes with your mind's natural processes, causing you to blank out, even on the questions you know well. The strain of testing during anxiety makes it difficult to stay focused, especially on a test that may take several hours. Extreme anxiety can take a huge mental toll, making it difficult not only to recall test information but even to understand the test questions or pull your thoughts together.

Review Video: How Test Anxiety Affects Memory
Visit mometrix.com/academy and enter code: 609003

Effects of Test Anxiety

Test anxiety is like a disease—if left untreated, it will get progressively worse. Anxiety leads to poor performance, and this reinforces the feelings of fear and failure, which in turn lead to poor performances on subsequent tests. It can grow from a mild nervousness to a crippling condition. If allowed to progress, test anxiety can have a big impact on your schooling, and consequently on your future.

Test anxiety can spread to other parts of your life. Anxiety on tests can become anxiety in any stressful situation, and blanking on a test can turn into panicking in a job situation. But fortunately, you don't have to let anxiety rule your testing and determine your grades. There are a number of relatively simple steps you can take to move past anxiety and function normally on a test and in the rest of life.

Review Video: How Test Anxiety Impacts Your Grades
Visit mometrix.com/academy and enter code: 939819

Physical Steps for Beating Test Anxiety

While test anxiety is a serious problem, the good news is that it can be overcome. It doesn't have to control your ability to think and remember information. While it may take time, you can begin taking steps today to beat anxiety.

Just as your first hint that you may be struggling with anxiety comes from the physical symptoms, the first step to treating it is also physical. Rest is crucial for having a clear, strong mind. If you are tired, it is much easier to give in to anxiety. But if you establish good sleep habits, your body and mind will be ready to perform optimally, without the strain of exhaustion. Additionally, sleeping well helps you to retain information better, so you're more likely to recall the answers when you see the test questions.

Getting good sleep means more than going to bed on time. It's important to allow your brain time to relax. Take study breaks from time to time so it doesn't get overworked, and don't study right before bed. Take time to rest your mind before trying to rest your body, or you may find it difficult to fall asleep.

Review Video: The Importance of Sleep for Your Brain
Visit mometrix.com/academy and enter code: 319338

Along with sleep, other aspects of physical health are important in preparing for a test. Good nutrition is vital for good brain function. Sugary foods and drinks may give a burst of energy but this burst is followed by a crash, both physically and emotionally. Instead, fuel your body with protein and vitamin-rich foods.

Also, drink plenty of water. Dehydration can lead to headaches and exhaustion, especially if your brain is already under stress from the rigors of the test. Particularly if your test is a long one, drink water during the breaks. And if possible, take an energy-boosting snack to eat between sections.

Review Video: How Diet Can Affect your Mood
Visit mometrix.com/academy and enter code: 624317

Along with sleep and diet, a third important part of physical health is exercise. Maintaining a steady workout schedule is helpful, but even taking 5-minute study breaks to walk can help get your blood pumping faster and clear your head. Exercise also releases endorphins, which contribute to a positive feeling and can help combat test anxiety.

When you nurture your physical health, you are also contributing to your mental health. If your body is healthy, your mind is much more likely to be healthy as well. So take time to rest, nourish your body with healthy food and water, and get moving as much as possible. Taking these physical steps will make you stronger and more able to take the mental steps necessary to overcome test anxiety.

Review Video: How to Stay Healthy and Prevent Test Anxiety
Visit mometrix.com/academy and enter code: 877894

Mental Steps for Beating Test Anxiety

Working on the mental side of test anxiety can be more challenging, but as with the physical side, there are clear steps you can take to overcome it. As mentioned earlier, test anxiety often stems from lack of preparation, so the obvious solution is to prepare for the test. Effective studying may be the most important weapon you have for beating test anxiety, but you can and should employ several other mental tools to combat fear.

First, boost your confidence by reminding yourself of past success—tests or projects that you aced. If you're putting as much effort into preparing for this test as you did for those, there's no reason you should expect to fail here. Work hard to prepare; then trust your preparation.

Second, surround yourself with encouraging people. It can be helpful to find a study group, but be sure that the people you're around will encourage a positive attitude. If you spend time with others who are anxious or cynical, this will only contribute to your own anxiety. Look for others who are motivated to study hard from a desire to succeed, not from a fear of failure.

Third, reward yourself. A test is physically and mentally tiring, even without anxiety, and it can be helpful to have something to look forward to. Plan an activity following the test, regardless of the outcome, such as going to a movie or getting ice cream.

When you are taking the test, if you find yourself beginning to feel anxious, remind yourself that you know the material. Visualize successfully completing the test. Then take a few deep, relaxing breaths and return to it. Work through the questions carefully but with confidence, knowing that you are capable of succeeding.

Developing a healthy mental approach to test taking will also aid in other areas of life. Test anxiety affects more than just the actual test—it can be damaging to your mental health and even contribute to depression. It's important to beat test anxiety before it becomes a problem for more than testing.

Review Video: Test Anxiety and Depression
Visit mometrix.com/academy and enter code: 904704

Study Strategy

Being prepared for the test is necessary to combat anxiety, but what does being prepared look like? You may study for hours on end and still not feel prepared. What you need is a strategy for test prep. The next few pages outline our recommended steps to help you plan out and conquer the challenge of preparation.

STEP 1: SCOPE OUT THE TEST

Learn everything you can about the format (multiple choice, essay, etc.) and what will be on the test. Gather any study materials, course outlines, or sample exams that may be available. Not only will this help you to prepare, but knowing what to expect can help to alleviate test anxiety.

STEP 2: MAP OUT THE MATERIAL

Look through the textbook or study guide and make note of how many chapters or sections it has. Then divide these over the time you have. For example, if a book has 15 chapters and you have five days to study, you need to cover three chapters each day. Even better, if you have the time, leave an extra day at the end for overall review after you have gone through the material in depth.

If time is limited, you may need to prioritize the material. Look through it and make note of which sections you think you already have a good grasp on, and which need review. While you are studying, skim quickly through the familiar sections and take more time on the challenging parts. Write out your plan so you don't get lost as you go. Having a written plan also helps you feel more in control of the study, so anxiety is less likely to arise from feeling overwhelmed at the amount to cover.

STEP 3: GATHER YOUR TOOLS

Decide what study method works best for you. Do you prefer to highlight in the book as you study and then go back over the highlighted portions? Or do you type out notes of the important information? Or is it helpful to make flashcards that you can carry with you? Assemble the pens, index cards, highlighters, post-it notes, and any other materials you may need so you won't be distracted by getting up to find things while you study.

If you're having a hard time retaining the information or organizing your notes, experiment with different methods. For example, try color-coding by subject with colored pens, highlighters, or post-it notes. If you learn better by hearing, try recording yourself reading your notes so you can listen while in the car, working out, or simply sitting at your desk. Ask a friend to quiz you from your flashcards, or try teaching someone the material to solidify it in your mind.

STEP 4: CREATE YOUR ENVIRONMENT

It's important to avoid distractions while you study. This includes both the obvious distractions like visitors and the subtle distractions like an uncomfortable chair (or a too-comfortable couch that makes you want to fall asleep). Set up the best study environment possible: good lighting and a comfortable work area. If background music helps you focus, you may want to turn it on, but otherwise keep the room quiet. If you are using a computer to take notes, be sure you don't have any other windows open, especially applications like social media, games, or anything else that could distract you. Silence your phone and turn off notifications. Be sure to keep water close by so you stay hydrated while you study (but avoid unhealthy drinks and snacks).

Also, take into account the best time of day to study. Are you freshest first thing in the morning? Try to set aside some time then to work through the material. Is your mind clearer in the afternoon or evening? Schedule your study session then. Another method is to study at the same time of day that you will take the test, so that your brain gets used to working on the material at that time and will be ready to focus at test time.

STEP 5: STUDY!

Once you have done all the study preparation, it's time to settle into the actual studying. Sit down, take a few moments to settle your mind so you can focus, and begin to follow your study plan. Don't give in to distractions or let yourself procrastinate. This is your time to prepare so you'll be ready to fearlessly approach the test. Make the most of the time and stay focused.

Of course, you don't want to burn out. If you study too long you may find that you're not retaining the information very well. Take regular study breaks. For example, taking five minutes out of every hour to walk briskly, breathing deeply and swinging your arms, can help your mind stay fresh.

As you get to the end of each chapter or section, it's a good idea to do a quick review. Remind yourself of what you learned and work on any difficult parts. When you feel that you've mastered the material, move on to the next part. At the end of your study session, briefly skim through your notes again.

But while review is helpful, cramming last minute is NOT. If at all possible, work ahead so that you won't need to fit all your study into the last day. Cramming overloads your brain with more information than it can process and retain, and your tired mind may struggle to recall even previously learned information when it is overwhelmed with last-minute study. Also, the urgent nature of cramming and the stress placed on your brain contribute to anxiety. You'll be more likely to go to the test feeling unprepared and having trouble thinking clearly.

So don't cram, and don't stay up late before the test, even just to review your notes at a leisurely pace. Your brain needs rest more than it needs to go over the information again. In fact, plan to finish your studies by noon or early afternoon the day before the test. Give your brain the rest of the day to relax or focus on other things, and get a good night's sleep. Then you will be fresh for the test and better able to recall what you've studied.

STEP 6: TAKE A PRACTICE TEST

Many courses offer sample tests, either online or in the study materials. This is an excellent resource to check whether you have mastered the material, as well as to prepare for the test format and environment.

Check the test format ahead of time: the number of questions, the type (multiple choice, free response, etc.), and the time limit. Then create a plan for working through them. For example, if you have 30 minutes to take a 60-question test, your limit is 30 seconds per question. Spend less time on the questions you know well so that you can take more time on the difficult ones.

If you have time to take several practice tests, take the first one open book, with no time limit. Work through the questions at your own pace and make sure you fully understand them. Gradually work up to taking a test under test conditions: sit at a desk with all study materials put away and set a timer. Pace yourself to make sure you finish the test with time to spare and go back to check your answers if you have time.

After each test, check your answers. On the questions you missed, be sure you understand why you missed them. Did you misread the question (tests can use tricky wording)? Did you forget the information? Or was it something you hadn't learned? Go back and study any shaky areas that the practice tests reveal.

Taking these tests not only helps with your grade, but also aids in combating test anxiety. If you're already used to the test conditions, you're less likely to worry about it, and working through tests until you're scoring well gives you a confidence boost. Go through the practice tests until you feel comfortable, and then you can go into the test knowing that you're ready for it.

Test Tips

On test day, you should be confident, knowing that you've prepared well and are ready to answer the questions. But aside from preparation, there are several test day strategies you can employ to maximize your performance.

First, as stated before, get a good night's sleep the night before the test (and for several nights before that, if possible). Go into the test with a fresh, alert mind rather than staying up late to study.

Try not to change too much about your normal routine on the day of the test. It's important to eat a nutritious breakfast, but if you normally don't eat breakfast at all, consider eating just a protein bar. If you're a coffee drinker, go ahead and have your normal coffee. Just make sure you time it so that the caffeine doesn't wear off right in the middle of your test. Avoid sugary beverages, and drink enough water to stay hydrated but not so much that you need a restroom break 10 minutes into the test. If your test isn't first thing in the morning, consider going for a walk or doing a light workout before the test to get your blood flowing.

Allow yourself enough time to get ready, and leave for the test with plenty of time to spare so you won't have the anxiety of scrambling to arrive in time. Another reason to be early is to select a good seat. It's helpful to sit away from doors and windows, which can be distracting. Find a good seat, get out your supplies, and settle your mind before the test begins.

When the test begins, start by going over the instructions carefully, even if you already know what to expect. Make sure you avoid any careless mistakes by following the directions.

Then begin working through the questions, pacing yourself as you've practiced. If you're not sure on an answer, don't spend too much time on it, and don't let it shake your confidence. Either skip it and come back later, or eliminate as many wrong answers as possible and guess among the remaining ones. Don't dwell on these questions as you continue—put them out of your mind and focus on what lies ahead.

Be sure to read all of the answer choices, even if you're sure the first one is the right answer. Sometimes you'll find a better one if you keep reading. But don't second-guess yourself if you do immediately know the answer. Your gut instinct is usually right. Don't let test anxiety rob you of the information you know.

If you have time at the end of the test (and if the test format allows), go back and review your answers. Be cautious about changing any, since your first instinct tends to be correct, but make sure you didn't misread any of the questions or accidentally mark the wrong answer choice. Look over any you skipped and make an educated guess.

At the end, leave the test feeling confident. You've done your best, so don't waste time worrying about your performance or wishing you could change anything. Instead, celebrate the successful

completion of this test. And finally, use this test to learn how to deal with anxiety even better next time.

Important Qualification

Not all anxiety is created equal. If your test anxiety is causing major issues in your life beyond the classroom or testing center, or if you are experiencing troubling physical symptoms related to your anxiety, it may be a sign of a serious physiological or psychological condition. If this sounds like your situation, we strongly encourage you to seek professional help.

Thank You

We at Mometrix would like to extend our heartfelt thanks to you, our friend and patron, for allowing us to play a part in your journey. It is a privilege to serve people from all walks of life who are unified in their commitment to building the best future they can for themselves.

The preparation you devote to these important testing milestones may be the most valuable educational opportunity you have for making a real difference in your life. We encourage you to put your heart into it—that feeling of succeeding, overcoming, and yes, conquering will be well worth the hours you've invested.

We want to hear your story, your struggles and your successes, and if you see any opportunities for us to improve our materials so we can help others even more effectively in the future, please share that with us as well. **The team at Mometrix would be absolutely thrilled to hear from you!** So please, send us an email (support@mometrix.com) and let's stay in touch.

> If you'd like some additional help, check out these other
> resources we offer for your exam:
> http://MometrixFlashcards.com/Series24

Additional Bonus Material

Due to our efforts to try to keep this book to a manageable length, we've created a link that will give you access to all of your additional bonus material.

Please visit https://www.mometrix.com/bonus948/series24 to access the information.